D0996988

EDDIE BRABEN'S

Morecambe & Wise

BOOK

10 9 8 7 6 5 4 3 2 1

First published in 2013 by Ebury Press, an imprint of Ebury Publishing

A Random House Group company

The Random House Group Limited Reg. No. 954009

Addresses for companies within the Random House Group can be found at www.randomhouse.co.uk

A CIP catalogue record for this book is available from the British Library

The Random House Group Limited supports the Forest Stewardship Council® (FSC®), the leading international forest-certification organisation. Our books carrying the FSC label are printed on FSC®-certified paper. FSC is the only forest-certification scheme supported by the leading environmental organisations, including Greenpeace. Our paper procurement policy can be found at www.randomhouse.co.uk/environment

Printed and bound in India by Replika Press Pvt. Ltd

Produced for Ebury Press by Essential Works
Designed for Essential Works by Barbara Doherty
www.essentialworks.co.uk

ISBN 9780091944995

To buy books by your favourite authors and register for offers visit www.randomhouse.co.uk

EDDIE BRABEN'S
Morecambe & Wise
BOOK

EBURY
PRESS

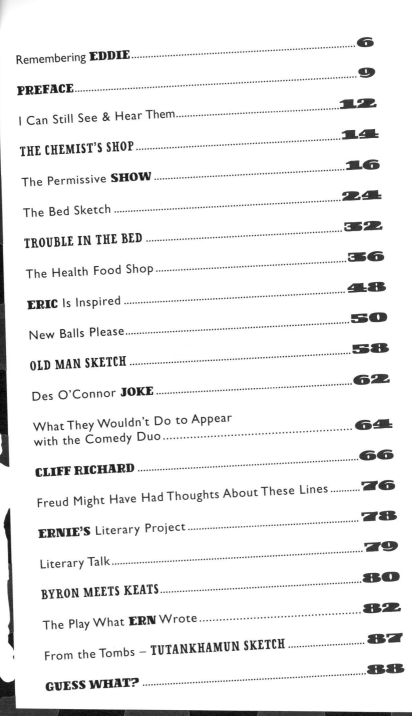

REMEMBERING EDDIE

BY DEE BRABEN

I AM REALLY PROUD to write this introduction for Eddie's new book. It's an honour.

Comedy writing was his life; he so loved to make people laugh. The deadlines and occasional days when ideas were very few could make it a chore but when the ideas started to flow that turned into immeasurable joy for millions of people.

When we were out having coffee or lunch at our local haunt he would often say to me, 'See that man, see that woman, they don't know it but at some time in their lives I have made them smile or possibly even laugh.' That's quite a legacy to leave.

Eddie's writing was inspired in his childhood and teenage years by a love of radio, music, books and the stars he often went to see at the Liverpool Empire – among them his particular favourites, Laurel & Hardy. Little could he have known then that he was undergoing a learning process that was to serve him so well in later life.

Eddie did so love his solitude. He always wrote alone, and often went on solitary long walks. Among his favourite were those taken near his retreat on the Llyn Peninsula, North Wales. With his head full of Jolly Robins (as he would say) off he'd go 'O'er bush and heath' with binoculars at the ready, stopping now and again to catch amazing views of curlews and skylarks or the stunning views over Cardigan Bay.

Occasionally our children would run down the winding country lane to catch him up by the little bridge, to play his version of Poohsticks – for which he made up the name of 'Yocko Me Tatty Bungle', which they would shout when they spotted their chosen crisp packet or toffee wrapper floating out from under the bridge. Doing silly things was

something of a speciality for Eddie – like pinching the stickers from the fruit in our local supermarket (sorry Mr. Spar). He needed them to decorate his walking stick. When we arrived home he would pull up the sleeve of his jumper and there they would be – stickers, all up his arm.

Most men would put notches on their walking sticks, but not Eddie; it had to be fruit stickers from around the world.

It was the long, long walks that were so important to him, though. They allowed him the tranquillity he needed in order to plan out the words that would bounce around in his head as he walked (he loved words).

The jokes and sketches would then be put on to paper for the next series, for whomever he would be writing for – and wow! What an array of stars there were: David Frost, Ronnie Corbett and Ken Dodd...

London and America tried to lure him away from Liverpool at one time but, as he once said to an American TV producer in 1971, 'I can't come now, I'm cooking chips for our tea.' I was in hospital at the time having our second daughter.

It was just as well that Eddie did decline that offer, because otherwise that special phone call from the late Bill Cotton of the BBC asking him to write for Morecambe and Wise would never have happened. When it did, it was a real surprise. Not many people know, but back then, he used to think that he wasn't capable of writing for Morecambe and Wise. Of course, as we all know now, Eddie couldn't have been more wrong.

All his love of the radio, books, poetry, music and of course his great gift for comedy writing, resulted in the creation of some of the best-loved and known classic comedy moments of British television history.

Eddie Braben was to Morecambe and Wise what Walt Disney was to Mickey Mouse.

It was hard watching him pound the typewriter for up to sixteen hours a day producing 13 shows plus the Christmas show every year, but with John Ammonds as producer, what a team they made. They have left us with all those joyful memories; the fun and the laughter that I'm sure will live on in generations for a long time.

In later years Eddie still wrote, for two hours in the morning and two hours in the afternoon – and non-stop for the rest of the day. He just had to write, he just wanted to make people laugh with his jokes, funny poems, new sketches or drawing comedy cards with humorous captions.

Putting this book together gave him immense satisfaction and I'm sure all the words on the following pages will bring a smile or perhaps a giggle because, as he would say, 'that's what life should be all about: FUN & LAUGHTER.'

PREFACE
BY EDDIE BRABEN

WHEN YOU'RE A writer you are rather like a literary chef. You go through the letters of the alphabet, select the ones that you might be able to do something with, mix them together to make the words that you like, and then roll them out in such a way that they make a decent read. Is that cool or what?

The object of a preface is to give the reader some idea as to what the book is about. Unfortunately I haven't read this book yet so you'll just have to turn the pages.

Some parts have been deleted as they do contain flash photography.

When I first took up the quill to put words to paper I was advised: 'Write only about what you know.' That was the worst piece of advice I was ever given. I ask you, how many people did Agatha Christie murder before she wrote her first mystery thriller? How many rabbit holes did Lewis Carroll have to fall down?

How many men did Jackie Collins ... I won't go on. I write about what I don't know, it's much more fun.

Although it's almost thirty years since I last wrote for Eric and Ern, I still can't stop comedy ideas from running around inside my head. I can see and hear them performing these new words and I don't want them to go untold. Comedy is to be enjoyed, which is why – in among the classics – I'll be dropping in the odd new comedy routine in this volume. Privileged? Yes, that's the word that I'm looking for.

A comedy duo like Morecambe and Wise happens just once in a lifetime, and I was privileged to have been around when it happened in mine, and continued for fourteen glorious and fun-filled years.

When I met them for the very first time in Bill Cotton's office at the BBC TV Centre in 1967, Bill at that time was head of Light Entertainment. I knew within minutes of that first meeting that this was the start of something special. It was very special, and went on to be what became known as the Golden Triangle. My thanks to whoever came up with that decorative phrase.

The magic of that first meeting stayed with me for fourteen unforgettable years.

It was an exciting comedy time when two middle-aged men, one with spectacles and the other with short, fat hairy legs, were so popular that on the night of 25 December 1977, 28,835,000 viewers turned their TV sets on to watch Eric and Ernie.

What was it about these two very ordinary, very unassuming men that captured the hearts and touched the funny bone of a nation and made them so unforgettable? Love would not be an exaggeration. What was that magic something with which they were blessed? I saw it at that first meeting and based all my future work for them on what I saw that day – innocence.

I combined that innocence with the natural warmth and affection that they had for each other and it produced comedy that didn't hurt or leave bruises.

Watch them as they do their hop and skip dance. Do you see what I see?

Two little boys enjoying life.

I sincerely hope that among the pages that follow, you will find the warmth and comforting glow of comedy sunshine.

I CAN STILL & HEAR THEM...

IT STILL HAPPENS, and I'm so grateful that it does. I get ideas for Eric and Ernie comedy routines even though they are no longer centre stage. Old habits, etc. ... I can't just let the ideas drift away; I have to put them on paper.

'Where did this come from?' asked my wife as she read the pages written in longhand that I'd asked her to print off. 'I haven't seen this before'.

I explained that was because I'd only just written it and nobody had read the words or seen them. It makes me smile because I can see and hear them performing this sketch. They would have had fun with it.

Eric and Ernie are centre stage, in front of the closed curtains.

Eric: Ern.

Ernie: Yes.

Eric: Good. When you left home tears were shed.

Ernie: True. Some folk were very upset when I left home.

Eric: An understatement. Snow White was heartbroken.

Ernie: I knew it. Look, just get on with whatever it is you're going to do.

Eric: Our writer's written a new sketch.

Ernie: You mean he's sober?

Eric: Make the most of it.

Ernie: What's it about?

Eric: It takes place in a chemist's shop.

Ernie: Is it any good?

Eric: It comes quite close to being almost not bad.

Ernie: We might as well do it because there's not much on telly.

Eric: What is on telly?

Ernie: Countdown.

Eric: Let's do it.

Ernie: Ladies and gentlemen, a new sketch set in a chemist's shop.

Eric: Why do they call it Boots?

Ernie: I've no idea

Eric: They don't sell laces.

Ernie: Are you sure Countdown is on TV?

Eric: Roads are gridlocked.

THE CHEMIST'S SHOP

UNSEEN!

A white-coated Ernie is behind the counter. Eric enters, as customer.

ERNIE   Good morning, sir.

ERIC   A pleasant enough day. Although the weatherman did warn that there was a depression moving down from the north. That could be the wife's mother coming to pay a visit.

ERNIE   How can I help you?

ERIC   You could pay off my mortgage. Cure my wife of her drink problem.

ERNIE   Not within my capabilities, sir.

ERIC   Or mine, really. Sorry, could I have a word with the chemist, please?

ERNIE   I am the pharmacist.

ERIC   What time will the chemist be in?

ERNIE   I am a chemist and a pharmacist.

ERIC   You buy one you get one free?

ERNIE   If you could tell me what the problem is, sir.

ERIC   Of course. A large swelling just below the big toe.

ERNIE   That would be a bunion, sir.

ERIC   Bunion, are you sure?

ERNIE   Positive.

ERIC   You've been most helpful. Thank you. *(Turns to leave the shop)*

ERNIE   Sir. I might have something that might cure your bunion.

ERIC   I haven't got a bunion.

ERNIE   But you said a large swelling just below the big toe.

ERIC   That was the clue. I couldn't find the answer to it in the crossword I'm doing. Thank you.

Eric leaves, Ern looks frustrated

THE PERMISSIVE SHOW

Eric and Ernie come front of stage for the opening sketch.

ERIC   What kind of a show is it tonight?

ERNIE   What kind of a show is it tonight?

ERIC   Well you can put it that way if you like.

ERNIE   It's our normal type of show, we're going to introduce some lovely …

ERIC   Is it?

ERNIE   Yes.

ERIC   Oh. Is it going to be one of those shows? I mean it's not going to upset anybody?

ERNIE   Certainly not.

ERIC   You leaving then? It's just a joke … only, I've been thinking – and that's painful – I've been thinking there's too much of it on television – you reckon?

ERNIE   Too much of it?

ERIC   I think so as well.

ERNIE   It?

ERIC   Yes. That word you can't say.

ERNIE   Oh, you mean sex!

ERIC   *(Gasps, slaps Ernie's cheeks then covers his mouth, looking sideways, mortified)* Yes, that's the word.

ERNIE: *(Pushing Eric away)* Well I can assure you and the viewers looking in that there'll be no sex on this show.

ERIC   No sex?

ERNIE   No.

ERIC   You realise what you've done, don't you?

ERNIE   What?

ERIC   You've lost us 99% of our viewing audience. Actually 100% because I'm leaving as well. *(Moves to leave stage, Ernie grabs his arm and pulls him back)*

ERNIE   What makes you think that we'd do that sort of show anyway?

ERIC   Ah well, Kenny Ball has been told that we are doing a permissive edition of our show tonight, for Welsh viewers.

ERNIE   For Welsh viewers? Permissive edition? There'll be nothing permissive in this show tonight.

ERIC   Wanna bet?

ERNIE   I do!

ERIC   Look over there at Kenny Ball, go on. *(Camera shows Kenny Ball and his Jazzmen naked, standing behind a white grand piano)*

ERIC   Horrifying isn't it?

ERNIE   Horrifying? That's disgusting!

17

ERIC   Looks like a butcher's shop.

ERNIE   How did that happen?

ERIC   Well evidently there was a note left on a hook in Kenny Ball's dressing room – well, that is his dressing room, actually.

ERNIE   Who was the note from?

ERIC   Nobody knows.

ERNIE   Anonymous?

ERIC   There was no name on it.

ERNIE   Well where's the note now?

ERIC   I have it here. *(Takes a piece of paper out of his pocket; there's a hole in it, through which Eric puts the tip of his nose)*

ERNIE   This is the note that was sent to Kenny Ball?

ERIC   That's the one.

ERNIE   *(Reading)* 'Dear Kenny, we are doing a very permissive show tonight …'

ERIC   That's true.

ERNIE   *(Continuing to read)* 'would appreciate it if you and the boys would appear with no clothes on. Signed, Hopeful. P.S. Must go now, Ern's waiting for me.'

ERIC   Ern's waiting for me, that's true.

ERNIE   Really! You sent this note.

ERIC   How could you tell?

ERNIE   Do you realise thousands of viewers saw Kenny Ball like that!

ERIC   Don't worry, they'll think it's an advert for a new dog meat.

ERNIE   Listen, I'm going to get to the bottom of this ...

ERIC   You would have done if you could move that piano, I tell you that!

ERNIE   There's too much of that stuff on television, this permissiveness, they ought to stop it.

ERIC   Of course there is. I can't stand seeing it myself.

ERNIE   Neither can I.

ERIC   Doing it is a different proposition, but seeing it ... no. Saw one the other night and it was horrifying.

ERNIE   Horrifying?

ERIC   Shocking. I couldn't believe my glasses.

ERNIE   If they're going to put things like that on television they should warn you beforehand.

ERIC   Of course they should – then I could find me glasses, couldn't I? Well, as I was saying, if I can just get a word in edgewise. I saw a play the other night, it was shocking, terrifying.

ERNIE   Really?

ERIC   I nearly dropped the au pair girl.

ERNIE   So what happened in this shocking play?

ERIC   I don't know if I can tell you about it.

ERNIE   Go on, tell me.

ERIC   Shall I? Otherwise we'll be here all night won't we? Alright, I'll tell you. What happened was, it opened on a street, there was this lamp, shining down on a wet pavement and there was a girl underneath it. What do you think of that?

ERNIE   That's ominous.

ERIC   Eh?

ERNIE   Ominous.

ERIC   I thought that.

ERNIE   Yes.

ERIC   Didn't know what it meant but I thought it. Now then, this fella walks towards her, and … I tell you what, it's better if I show you. You play the part of the girl, and as I walk by, you say, 'Hello, Big Boy!'

ERNIE   'Hello Big Boy'. I've got it.

ERIC   No, no don't say that, 'cos he's no fool, this fella. He knows she's got it. The lamplight and everything … are you ready?

ERNIE   I'm ready.

ERIC   I'm walking by, are you looking? *(Eric minces up to Ernie)* I'm walking …

ERNIE   Hello, Big Boy.

Eric strangles Ernie.

ERNIE   *(Pushing Eric off)* What did you do that for?

ERIC   Ah well, you see, he hates women. And it's the only chance I'll get to have a go at you …

ERNIE   But what was this thing that was so disgusting about it on the television?

ERIC   I'm coming to it.

ERNIE   Alright.

ERIC   It's his brother. There's this love affair between this man and this woman.

ERNIE   That's normal.

ERIC   Wanna bet? What happens is it opens in a supermarket and this woman's bending over a deep freezer …

ERNIE   Oh-ho-ho! *(He winks and leers at Eric)*

ERIC   Now then, she drops her shopping basket, this man walks in and treads on one of her plums. Now that upsets her.

ERNIE   I bet it did.

ERIC   There's only seven to a pound, you see. He, being a gentleman, picks up the basket and she takes him back to her flat. Lets them both in with a key, takes off her raincoat – and what's she got on underneath?

ERNIE   Nothing!

ERIC   *(Slaps Ernie's cheeks)* Great. Starkers!

ERNIE   Starkers?

ERIC   The full Graham Starkers.

ERNIE   I know. Nothing on at all!

ERIC   What's that word again?

ERNIE   Sex. *(Eric slaps his cheeks)*

ERIC   Now, he doesn't know where to look, but eventually he finds a place. She dives into his arms, looks over his shoulder and says, 'What lovely teeth you've got'. I didn't follow that at all.

ERNIE   Neither do I.

ERIC   No, I don't think the author did either. So suddenly he lifts her up in his arms …

ERNIE   Yes … ?

ERIC   Goes over to the bed …

ERNIE   Yes … ?

ERIC   Throws her on the bed, raises his hat, jumps out of the window in the pouring rain, singing 'Hot chocolate, drinking chocolate, hot chocolate, drinking chocolate'.

ERNIE   'Hot chocolate, drinking chocolate?'

ERIC   'Hot chocolate, drinking chocolate', yes.

ERNIE   But that's the commercial!

ERIC   Eh?

ERNIE   That is the commercial.

ERIC   I thought it was a funny ending. I've seen six plays with that ending. I've always switched off after that and gone to bed. Switched off, anyway …

THE BED SKETCH

I HAVE ALWAYS ENJOYED writing and watching the performances of the flat sketches, particularly bed sketches. The thinking behind placing Eric and Ernie in a double bed was simply that there was no escape. They could speak their innermost thoughts, taunt, jibe and insult each other – something that they would never, never, ever do in front of anyone else.

Some of my favourite lines first made themselves known in bed sketches. Eric looking out of the window and observing, 'Red sky at night means that the shepherd's cottage is on fire.' Still looking out and upwards from the window, 'That's Mars up there, you can see it between meals.' Or the time when a police car went speeding past with its siren sounding, 'He's not going to sell much ice cream going at that speed'.

In one of the very earliest bed sketches, Eric was reading *The Wind in the Willows* while Ern was creating another masterpiece, his fourteenth that day. After the recording and while still in the bed, Eric wrote inside the book, 'To Eddie. Stolen from BBC Props. June 1979.' I really can't tell you how much that beautiful book means to me.

We did once have a gag in a bed sketch which I believe was taken out on the grounds that it might have upset animal lovers. If you're an animal lover, look away now.

IF YOU'RE AN ANIMAL LOVER, LOOK AWAY

ERIC I've put the cat out.

ERNIE What for?

ERIC It was on fire.

ERIC It's got me beat, I just can't make it out. Just can't understand it at all. The market's down four points.

ERIC Got me beat as well. Desperate Dan's just eaten four cow pies – he's still hungry.

ERNIE What are you talking about?

ERIC In this comic he is, every week. He's just stopped a train with his chin.

ERNIE Why don't you grow up? I'm trying to study big business.

ERIC A little less lust for money and more fun, that's what we want in the world today.

ERNIE So we both read comics and who looks after the financial side of the business? Who pays the bills?

ERIC Lend me your pen.

Grabs Ernie's pen.

ERNIE No, I'm using it.

ERIC You can borrow mine. I want to join the dots up in this comic.

ERNIE Join what dots up?

ERIC *(Drawing on comic)* You join all the dots up and it makes a picture.

ERNIE   That must be very difficult.

ERIC   Not really. I do it every week. Wonder what the picture will be? *(Looks at picture)* That's disgusting, that is. Comics haven't half changed since I was a lad.

ERNIE   Don't you think that it's about time you grew up and accepted your responsibilities?

ERIC   *(Picks up a second comic)* Few more Peter Pans like me and the world would be a happier place.

ERNIE   Then you read your comics and leave me to attend to business matters.

ERIC   Great story in this comic, a topping yarn it says here.

ERNIE   You read it if it's all that topping.

ERIC   *(Reading aloud)* Dick D'Arcy stood before the headmaster of St Jim's. 'I give you my word of honour, sir,' he said with his head held high and firmness in his voice. 'I have no earthly idea how Matron's knickers came to be in my school bag.'

ERNIE   Disgusting. It doesn't say anything like that. Now shut up and leave me to work in peace. I'm engrossed in high finance.

ERIC   High finance.

ERNIE   Yes.

ERIC   With those legs? Impossible. I've been with you when you've gone into the bank, your little head just sticking up over the top of the counter and all the bank clerks whispering to one another – 'Sooty's back'.

ERNIE   Can I get on with my work?

ERIC   Call that work? Don't need brains for that.

ERNIE   In that case *you* should find it very easy.
You sort out the financial side of things.

ERIC   I'm busy aren't I?

ERNIE   Reading comics? Ha! You're as thick as a docker's sandwich.

ERIC   And what does that mean?

ERNIE   It means that I know. It means don't try and bluff me. We
went to the same school, we were in the same class – *I*
know.

ERIC   We're off now are we? Here we go again. 'All Our
Yesterdays'. Milverton Street School again?

ERNIE   Yes, Milverton Street.

ERIC   Keep bringing that one up when it suits you.

ERNIE   You're the one making the noise about brains.

ERIC   Gold stars I got in my sum book off 'Miss'.

ERNIE   You used to nick them out of her desk at playtime and stick
them in yourself.

ERIC:	I didn't. Miss gave them to me. Full of ticks it was, and VGs and nine out of ten.
ERNIE	I saw what she wrote in your book – she wrote, 'You must try harder'.
ERIC	That was nothing to do with sums – that was personal between me and Miss. You were the laughing stock of the class. No wonder I went up to 1A and you went down to 4C.
ERIC:	Read your paper.
ERNIE	We couldn't wait for Miss to get you to stand up and answer questions. 'Morecambe, where do we get demerara sugar from?' Do you remember what you said? 'From the Co-op, Miss'. *(Laughing)* Oh, dear me.
ERIC	What about PT then? What about PT, matie! Every time we had PT there was that note again from your mother. 'Please excuse Ernest from PT. He has a weak chest and mustn't take his vest off.'
ERNIE	That's not my fault. Not my fault if I had a weak chest.
ERIC	It couldn't have been all that weak.
ERNIE	What do you mean?
ERIC	I've kept this to myself all these years, but now that the knives are out and fully honed …
ERNIE	Go on.
ERIC	I saw you one playtime behind the bike shed with Rita Greenhough.
ERNIE	You never saw me behind the bike shed with Rita Greenhough.
ERIC	It was after that, that I had to start wearing glasses.
ERNIE	You never saw me behind the bike shed with Rita Greenhough.

I'M BUSY, AREN'T I?

READING COMICS? HA! YOU'RE AS THICK AS A DOCKER'S SANDWICH

ERIC   I met her last week and she was still laughing.

ERNIE   You never saw me behind the bike shed with Rita Greenhough. Jealous.

ERIC   What!?

ERNIE   You were jealous of me at school because I was always better dressed than you.

ERIC   Ha! Ha! You only started wearing long trousers when your dad went on nights.

ERNIE   At least my father didn't come home at night and knock my mother about.

ERIC   Your father didn't dare knock your mother about. Who'd want to tackle King Kong in a pinny?

ERNIE   This all started just because you know nothing about money matters and investments.

ERIC   Who doesn't know anything about investments?

ERNIE   You don't.

ERIC   I'll show you. *(Takes paper from Ernie)* If you want to invest your money put it in 'Ickey'.

ERNIE   Ickey? ICI *(Takes paper back from Eric)* Now please, a little peace and quiet? I'm meeting my bank manager in the morning to discuss investments.

ERIC   You carry on.

Ernie studies the Financial Times.

ERNIE   EMI looks good.

ERIC   Can't go wrong there.

ERNIE   What do you know about it? You don't even know what EMI stands for.

ERIC   I do.

ERNIE   What?

ERIC   Eric Morecambe's Irresistible.

ERNIE   Read your comic.

ERIC   Why this sudden interest in stocks and shares and investments all of a sudden? What's wrong with the biscuit tin under the bed?

ERNIE   Read your comic.

ERIC   *(Thinks for a second then picks up the* Beano*)* Lord Snooty. *(Laughs)* He's staying with his Aunt Agatha and she's just said to him will … *(Looks up)* You had an Aunt Agatha. She died about two months ago, didn't she?

ERNIE   It's got nothing to do with you – that's family business.

ERIC   *(Slowly realising)* Oooh! A little tickly did you have, eh! Come on. Let's have the truth.

ERNIE   If you must know, I've had a windfall.

ERIC	There's some bicarb in the cupboard. She's left you a few bob then?
ERNIE	There was a great affection between us – it was a terrible shock to me.
ERIC	You couldn't stand the sight of her.
ERNIE	Loved my auntie, I did.
ERIC	Crawler!
ERNIE	I didn't crawl at all! You've got to look after yourself in this life.
ERIC	You must be worth a few bob now then?
ERNIE	That's my business.
ERIC	How much did she leave you?
ERNIE	I'm not saying.
ERIC	Would you like a piece of my chicken sandwich?
ERNIE	No. You're not getting any of the money.
ERIC	You can have the whole of my chicken sandwich if you like, and this glass of milk.

Passes them over to Ernie, who takes them.

ERNIE	You're not getting any of the money so there's no point in trying to be nice to me. It doesn't suit you.
ERIC	All right, if that's your attitude I'm going to sleep. Good night.

He settles down under the covers. Ernie starts to drink the glass of milk; it sprays out either side.

ERNIE	You rotten devil!

Eric quietly sniggers to himself.

UNSEEN!

Trouble iN THE BED

THE FIRST BED sketch that I ever wrote for the boys caused a major problem. They read it to producer John Ammonds and the rehearsal room at Delgano Way, just behind Wormwood Scrubs Prison, echoed to the sound of their joint laughter and I was happy, but not for very long.

'That is funny' said Eric, as he put the script down and wiped away a laughter tear. Ernie agreed, then surprised me. No, he stunned me when he said, 'But we can't do it.'

Eric explained their problem. 'Two men in a bed together is too controversial.'

John Ammonds tried to rescue the bed by pointing out that this was Eric and Ernie, not two strangers.

No, they weren't convinced. Bill Cotton, bless him, he tried but the boys still did not like the idea.

I tried and tried and kept getting knocked back with my bed sketch.

The breakthrough came when I said to them both, 'If it's good enough for Laurel and Hardy it's good enough for you.'

Eric and Ernie looked at each other before Eric said, 'We'll do it.'

I think I might have shouted 'Hallelujah!'

The bed sketch that follows is quite recent. I'm letting it loose for the first time.

Eric is reading a book of film stars' biographies.
Ern is writing in a notebook. He pauses and looks thoughtful.

ERNIE   I'm thinking of taking a holiday.

ERIC   Anywhere in mind?

ERNIE   Switzerland.

ERIC   Very nice Switzerland. Full of Alps.

ERNIE   I've got the brochures.

ERIC   Try putting your head between your knees and drinking a glass of water. It works for me.

ERNIE   I've been thinking about it a lot lately.

ERIC   Are we still talking about Switzerland? It's a good country to go to for a holiday because of the exchange rate.

ERNIE   What is the exchange rate?

ERIC   In Switzerland you get thirty yodels to the pound. If you went on holiday to Wales you'd only get twenty-five ferfechans to the pound.

ERNIE   It's hopeless trying to hold a sensible conversation with you.

ERIC   That's true. In this film book that I'm reading it tells you all about famous film stars.

ERNIE   *(Writing, and not interested)* Good.

ERIC   The films they've made, how old they are. Remember Lassie?

ERNIE   Lassie the dog? I remember the film *Lassie Come Home,* that was a great film.

ERIC   You won't believe this Ern.

ERNIE   What?

ERIC   Lassie is now eighty-seven.

ERNIE   That did it. Good night. *(Ernie turns over)*

ERIC   SNOW WHITE'S 94, ERN. SHE SENDS HER REGARDS.

ERNIE   Good night! *(Ernie switches the light off)*

ERIC   Rotten devil! How can I annoy you with the light out.

ERNIE   I didn't get a wink of sleep last night because of you.

ERIC   Didn't you?

ERNIE   No. Do me a favour – don't have Windsor soup again before you go to bed.

ERIC   Why not?

ERNIE   You were out of bed last night four times, whistling the National Anthem.

ERIC   You were lucky I didn't have cock-a-leekie then.

THE HEALTH
FOOD SHOP

ERNIE WAS THE inspirational spark that brought this sketch to life.

He was one of the fittest I ever worked with, as fit as a boarding-house flea. He was a good tennis player, a very strong swimmer, played a lot of cricket and really did love sailing his boat.

ERIC'S FAVOURITE OUTDOOR HOBBY

BIRD WATCHING

Eric's favourite outdoor hobby was one we both shared: bird watching. One morning we both went o'er bush and heath, Eric raised his binoculars very high and said, 'Write this down quick!' I was really excited: 'What is it?' He replied, 'A great big pole tied down with two thick wires.' Needless to say that, before the expedition was over, Eric had also sighted Percy Thrower with a suitcase strapped to his legs flying south for the winter. He also saw a kestrel. When in my surprise I said, 'Good Lord,' Eric said, 'No, I can't see him.'

During a conversation with Ernie on the merits of healthy foods, he asked me what it was that helped me to relax. I told him 'Delius.' Ern looked rather puzzled then asked, 'Is that powder or liquid?' How could I not write a health food sketch?

Eric is seated alone in the flat watching television; from the TV set we hear fanfare and voice of Hughie Green.

VOICE   And now friends it's 'Make your mind up time.'

ERIC   I have … *(Quickly switches off and rises)* It's obvious who's going to win it this week – it'll be that eighty-eight-year-old lady from Cheltenham playing 'Sonny Boy' on the watering can. If she doesn't it'll be the Chelsea Pensioner who did the splits over the live lobster. I don't know where he gets them from. I wish Ernie would hurry up at the supermarket. I'm starving. I wouldn't mind betting that he's met that fellow doing the soap commercial for the television, offering Ern two big ones for his little one – he won't swap. He's a good lad, Ernie, he's gone out for those groceries without a murmur. I don't know what I'd do without him … buy a hamster probably.

Door to flat is kicked from the outside. Ernie cannot open the door as he has his hands full of groceries; he calls out.

ERNIE   Are you in there, Eric?!

ERIC   I don't know. I'll have to look. *(Looks inside jacket)* Yes, I am!

ERNIE   Come on, open up!

Eric moves towards the door and opens it. Ernie staggers in under the weight of a large cardboard box full of groceries.

ERNIE   This lot's heavy.

ERIC   Did you get the groceries?

ERNIE   Give me a hand.

ERIC   You shouldn't be carrying heavy things like that. You'll displace it again.

ERNIE   Don't just stand there. *(Puts box on settee)*

ERIC   What took you so long?

ERNIE   I met that fellow who offered me two big ones for my little one.

ERIC   You didn't swap, did you?

ERNIE   No, I didn't.

ERIC   I knew you wouldn't. Come on.

Eric helps Ernie to lower the box.

ERNIE   Any telephone calls for me while I was out?

ERIC   A director rang from Hollywood. Alfred somebody.

ERNIE   Hitchcock?

ERIC   He might have, I didn't ask.

ERNIE   He wants a thriller from me.

ERIC   Some hopes … What have you got, I'm starving.

ERNIE   Plenty here.

ERIC   Good lad. *(Looks into box … takes out packet)* That's all I needed.

ERNIE   What's wrong?

ERIC   You've been there again, haven't you?

ERNIE   Been where?

ERIC   That flaming health food shop. That's the fourth time this week. I hate health foods. I'm up to here with wheatgerm; if I go out I blow away in the breeze. And if I eat another starch-reduced roll and turn over in bed I'll crack.

ERNIE   Do you good this stuff will. You can't beat Mother Nature. Health foods build you up and make you strong. Give us a hand with this table.

Moves table in front of settee. They sit on settee. Eric looks at tin from box.

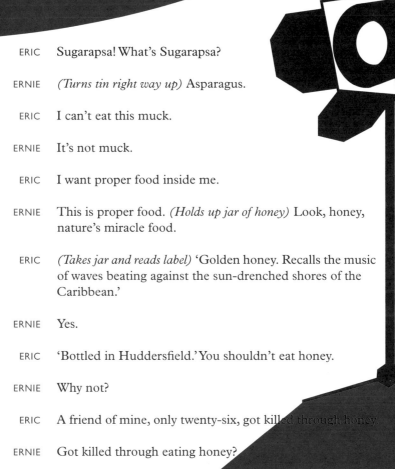

ERIC   Sugarapsa! What's Sugarapsa?

ERNIE   *(Turns tin right way up)* Asparagus.

ERIC   I can't eat this muck.

ERNIE   It's not muck.

ERIC   I want proper food inside me.

ERNIE   This is proper food. *(Holds up jar of honey)* Look, honey, nature's miracle food.

ERIC   *(Takes jar and reads label)* 'Golden honey. Recalls the music of waves beating against the sun-drenched shores of the Caribbean.'

ERNIE   Yes.

ERIC   'Bottled in Huddersfield.' You shouldn't eat honey.

ERNIE   Why not?

ERIC   A friend of mine, only twenty-six, got killed through honey.

ERNIE   Got killed through eating honey?

ERIC   Yes, a crate fell on his head. Take that rubbish back to the shop and get a couple of thick steaks and a few pounds of sausages. I've got to keep me strength up.

ERNIE   We eat far too much these days. We only need fourteen hundred calories to stay healthy and I'm going to keep fit with nature foods and plenty of exercise. *(He gets up)*

ERIC   Right. I'll fetch your lead.

(Ernie exercises)

ERIC   Don't overdo it, will you.

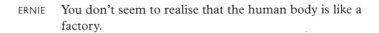

ERNIE   You don't seem to realise that the human body is like a factory.

ERIC   Oh. Are you on short time? Is the delicatessen shop still open?

ERNIE   And a lot of good the stuff they sell will do you.

ERIC   Mouthwatering some of the things they have hanging from the ceiling in that shop. I'm never sure whether it's food or somebody coming through the roof.

ERNIE   Not for me. I once had some snails from there.

ERIC   Took you six weeks to get to the bathroom. I might nip out to Wimpy's.

ERNIE   What for?

ERIC   A plate of Wimps.

ERNIE   Why don't you give this health food a try? You might even like it.

ERIC   *(Holding up a packet)* Puffed wheat – what are you trying to do to me? When I think of some of those meals we used to have at home when I was a lad. On a Sunday we'd have a roast duck – if the park was open.

ERNIE   *(Getting up)* Revolting that is.

ERIC   I take it then that you're deadly serious about nature and good health?

ERNIE   Never more so.

ERIC   Sit down and take the weight off your lavender bags.

Ernie sits on settee.

ERNIE   Well?

ERIC	You're serious about keeping healthy nature's way?
ERNIE	I've told you I am.
ERIC	Go the whole hog – join a nudist camp.
ERNIE	Me become a nudist?
ERIC	They'd let you join at a reduced price.
ERNIE	No, I couldn't go around with no clothes on.
ERIC	Well, take your cap in case you go shopping.
ERNIE	I couldn't become a nudist and that's final.
ERIC	*(Getting up)* Well, then that proves that you're only half-hearted about this whole nature business.
	Goes to put coat on.
ERNIE	Where are you going?
ERIC	We're both going to take this lot back to the health shop, get our money back and buy some proper food.
	Eric and Ernie enter the health food shop carrying the cardboard box.
ERNIE	Put the box down. *(Both lower box)* I'll show you, I'll show you just how good health foods are for you. *(Looking round)* There's nobody about.
ERIC	They're all dead. You make me laugh the way you get these crazes every so often. Last week it was 'Men's Lib' and you set fire to your braces.
ERNIE	Say what you like. I'm going to keep myself in good trim.
ERIC	You sound like a wick. There's one of those keep-fit bikes.

Eric climbs on to bike and pedals.

ERNIE   Just you get off that bike.

ERIC   Saddle's a bit small. Put the colour back in my cheeks.

Eric gets off bike.

ERNIE   The man will be here in a minute.

Man appears behind the counter.

MAN   I'm sorry to have kept you, I …

ERIC   *(From bike)* Can you tell me the way to Aberdeen?

Moves to counter.

MAN   Hello, Mr Wise.

ERNIE   Hello, Mr Warmsley.

MAN   Back for more of our health-giving products?

ERNIE   One has to look after oneself, Mr Warmsley.

MAN   Indeed. Early to bed, early to rise …

ERIC   Makes you a miser just like Ernie Wise. A quarter of gumdrops and two tins of bacon please. And we'd like our money back for this rubbish that you sold my friend.

ERNIE   Mr Warmsley, I'd like you to meet my friend.

MAN   Your friend. I see.

ERNIE   I'm afraid that he doesn't believe in the health-giving properties of nature foods.

MAN   My dear fellow. You must read some of our literature.

ERIC   Got any nudists' books?

MAN   We don't stock that sort of thing. This might enlighten you as to our products.

Hands Eric a leaflet.

ERIC   *(Looks at leaflet)* What does this say?

MAN   *(Looks at leaflet)* Get rid of acne.

ERIC   That's not nice – my auntie lives there.

ERNIE   Excuse me. *(Crosses Eric)* You'll have a job trying to convince him, Mr Warmsley.

MAN   We can but try, Mr erm …

ERIC   McQueen, Steve McQueen.

MAN   Well, Mr McQueen.

ERIC   You can call me Steve. I'm half a star.

ERNIE   Excuse me. *(Crosses)* Mr Warmsley is a wonderful advertisement for health foods. Tell him, Mr Warmsley.

ERIC   Yes, tell me, Mr Warmsley.

MAN   I've been on health foods for over twenty years now. Let me tell you something.

ERIC   Yes.

MAN   Many years ago before reading about nature's foods I was always a little queer.

ERIC   There's no answer to that.

ERNIE   Tell him what the specialist said, Mr Warmsley.

ERIC   Yes, tell me what the specialist said, Mr Warmsley.

MAN   I was for ever feeling unwell and off-colour, no energy, listless.

ERIC   And?

MAN   I placed myself in the hands of a health food specialist. The first thing he did was to cut off my carbohydrates.

I MIGHT NIP OUT TO WiMPY'S

WHAT FOR?

A PLATE OF WiMPS

ERIC   *(Grabs him)* Just watch it. This is a family show!

MAN   I've got orders to prepare for genuine clients. I'll send somebody else out to attend to you. *(Exits)*

ERIC   Are we going to buy some real food now?

ERNIE   No, I'm still convinced that health foods are best.

ERIC   Suit yourself. *(Sees vibrator)* What's this contraption?

ERNIE   Helps you lose weight.

ERIC   *(Puts the belt around waist)* Have I lost any?

ERNIE   Switch it on. *(Switches belt on)*

ERIC   Oooh! By golly it doesn't half go … me kneecaps are working loose … me jockey shorts are up around me neck … switch it off!!

ERNIE   *(Switches it off)* What do you think?

I'll tell you something. I'm frightened to stamp me foot.

I wonder where Mr Warmsley's got to?

Girl enters behind counter.

GIRL   Can I help you?

ERIC   Good Lord, Mr Warmsley, that was a quick change.

GIRL   Hello, Mr Wise. I've got your tablets.

Hands bottle to Ernie.

ERNIE   Thank you.

ERIC   *(Takes tablets)* Hello, what are these for? Give me those. *(Looks at label)* Nurse Lusty's Virility Tablets?

ERNIE   Yes, they're mine. *(To girl)* Do I take them before or after?

ERIC   Instead of. For a Plentitude of Power? Fortifies the over-forties, fractures the over-fifties. Puts you in fine fettle for it? Puts you in fine fettle for what?

ERNIE   Give me those tablets.

ERIC   Did you get these for him?

GIRL   Mr Wise did order them.

ERIC   You dirty little devil. No wonder you've been getting hot flushes. They're from Northern Spain – they give these to stallions. He's not having these, I'm responsible for him.

ERNIE   I'm over age.

ERIC   But undersized. Two of these and you'd disappear completely. They could be dangerous.

GIRL   They've done my husband a power of good.

ERIC   Husband?

GIRL   Cyril. Twenty-five years of age and no energy at all till he tried those tablets.

ERNIE He's been taking them, has he? *(Moves to the door)* By the way, how are the children?

GIRL The quads are doing very well and the triplets start school next month.

A very jaded old man appears in the door leaning on a walking stick.

MAN Hello, my dear.

ERIC Is this your father?

GIRL No, Cyril – my husband.

ERIC Cyril? *(To Ernie)* Quick, I'm taking you home.

They exit.

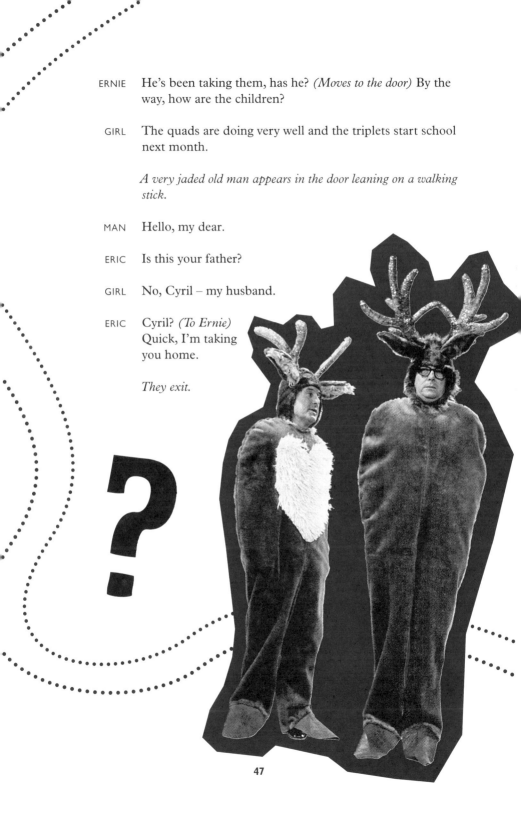

Eric: Ern, you are inspirational.

Ernie: Who have I inspired?

Eric: Me.

Ernie: You? You seriously think that you can write? You couldn't leave a note for the milkman.

Eric: Not like you to be so hurtful, Ern. You shouldn't say things like that when you haven't even heard any of my poems.

Ernie: You've written poetry?

Eric: Here's one of my poems that I've dedicated to my dear old grandad.

Ernie: That's nice. I'd like to hear your grandad poem.

Eric: Very well. There's a pair of empty trousers hanging up behind the door. They belong to dear old grandad. He's in the woman's house next door.

Ernie: That is the most obnoxious piece of poetry that I have ever heard.

Eric: I knew you'd like it. As you will this. Jack and Jill...

Ernie: We've all heard the Jack and Jill poem.

Eric: Not this version. When Jack and Jill went up the hill
they didn't go for a pail of water, they went and hid
behind a bush and did what they shouldn't oughter.

Ernie: Gerroff!

Eric: Thank you.

ERIC TELL ME something

YES ERNIE

ERIC DID YOU COME HERE
TONIGHT IN that hat?

YES ERNIE

ERIC COULDN'T YOU
GET A TAXI?

NEW BALLS PLEASE

IT WAS A great personal tragedy and an enormous disappointment for the nation when Eric Morecambe had to withdraw from the 1960 Olympic Games in Rome with a dislocated fetlock. That this great athlete would not be competing had deprived Great Britain of at least six gold medals, so he told me. He had good reason to feel bitter after the punishing training he had committed himself to, specially for the high jump. Every morning he had been preparing for this event in a field behind his Harpenden home. He took a 200-yard run with the pole, then leapt into the air, on occasions reaching a height of 60 feet. Shortly after making one of these prestigious jumps he said, 'Even if I don't win a gold medal, I should be able to get into Wembley to see the Cup Final without a ticket.' As a swimmer he is without doubt the best, so he told me. He was determined to become a swimmer, despite the setback at a very early age when a spectator shouted, as Eric dived into the water, 'Who threw those braces in?' As a tennis player, Eric's style was breathtakingly unique, copied by the greatest players in the world, including that lady legend of the courts, Jelly Bean King, so he told me. He was quite thrilled at doing a tennis sketch because, as he said at the time, 'This should prove an inspiration to all youngsters just starting out in the game.' Can anyone doubt that statement? Here is a ball-by-ball replay of what was arguably one of the greatest tennis matches ever screened by the BBC, as Eric takes on his great friend and rival, Ernie Wise.

It should be said that Ernie Wise was no pushover. He was a very fine player who once reached the final of the men's singles mixed doubles for women, so he told me. Credit where credit is due. When the tennis racket is spun to decide who serves, and it breaks, this was Eric's idea. When it came to the question of what to wear it was never asked because we all knew, no matter what the sketch was about, that Eric would wear his beloved suspenders. If you don't want to know the result of the pulsating match, look away or whitewash the cat.

Scene: A tennis court, of which we only see the half to the right-hand side of the net. Ernie is waiting with rackets. Eric enters through gate in long shorts.

ERNIE   Lovely day for it, Eric.

ERIC   Never mind that, just get on with the game.

ERNIE   Going to show me a thing or two are you?

ERIC   Cut the chat and let's get the game going.

Ernie tests the strings on his racket.

ERIC   What are you doing?

ERNIE   Testing the strings.

Eric tests his strings. They are very loose.

ERNIE   Good racket you've got there.

ERIC   I'll use me championship racket.

ERNIE   That's your championship racket.

ERIC   Annihilated them all in me time.

ERNIE   Like who?

ERIC   The greatest ever.

ERNIE   Who was that?

ERIC   Only Lew Grade.

ERNIE   Lew Hoad.

ERIC   He's changed his name again to protect the innocent! Where's the barley water?

ERNIE	You don't need barley water, this is just a friendly game.
ERIC	I don't play friendly games. I'm known as the killer of the court.
ERNIE	I can see that I'm going to have quite a game.
ERIC	Just get down there and whip a few up. I'll take it easy to begin with.
ERNIE	You'll take it easy.
ERIC	I won't belt them back at you at the start, give you a chance to get used to my speed of return.
ERNIE	Shall I serve or will you?
ERIC	Fine.
ERNIE	I'll spin the racket.
ERIC	Heads.
ERNIE	Heads?

Ernie spins Eric's racket; it falls on the ground and breaks into pieces.

ERNIE	I'll serve.
ERIC	You've broken my racket.
ERNIE	Use this one. *(Hands Eric a racket)* It's a wonder to me that you've never played Wimbledon.
ERIC	What's that got to do with tennis? Get down there and whip a few up.
ERNIE	Ready?
ERIC	Any time you like, sunshine.

Eric crouches, waiting for Ernie's serve. After a couple of seconds the ball flashes past Eric.

ERIC   *(Still crouched)* You can whip one up as soon as you like.

Ernie appears at his side of the net; beckons to Eric. Eric goes up to the net.

ERNIE   Fifteen love.

ERIC   What are you talking about?

ERNIE   I have got one past you. *(Points to ball at back of Eric's side of the court)* Fifteen love.

ERIC   *(Looks at the tennis ball)* That was there before, that was.

ERNIE   Fifteen love. *(With contempt)* Lew Grade. I'll serve a bouncy one.

ERIC   I don't like bouncy ones. You belt them as hard as you like.

ERNIE   Very well.

Ernie goes out of shot to his side of the court. Eric crouches, waiting.

ERNIE   Ready?

ERIC   I'm ready. This time you won't even see it when I belt it back. Just a white blur if you're lucky. *(Ern's serve flashes past Eric)* Any time you like and as hard as you like.

Ernie appears at his side of the net; beckons to Eric. Eric goes up to the net.

ERNIE   Thirty love.

ERIC   Thirty love what?

ERNIE   Thirty love. Just belted another one past you, you didn't even move.

ERIC   I was talking, wasn't I?

ERNIE   You've never stopped talking since we came on this court. You've never stopped boasting about how good you are.

ERIC   What chance do I stand when I'm playing against someone who cheats?

ERNIE   Thirty love.

ERIC   *(Very determined)* Right then, matie. Forearm smash you'll get now.

ERNIE   You're good at the forearm smash then?

FIFTEEN LOVE

I HAVE GOT ONE PAST YOU

WHAT ARE YOU TALKING ABOUT?

THAT WAS THERE BEFORE, THAT WAS

ERIC   Who do you think taught the forearm smash to Yvonne Dinnergong? I'll destroy you now matie.

ERNIE   Thirty love.

Ernie goes off to his side of the court.

ERNIE   Ready?

ERIC   You'll find out how ready I am.

Eric crouches, waiting and swaying slightly from side to side. After a long pause the ball flashes past him. Ernie appears at the net and beckons to Eric. Eric goes to the net.

ERNIE   Forty love.

ERIC   What kind of a way do you call that to play tennis?

ERNIE   Quite within the rules – serve in my own time and if you're not ready it's hardly my fault. Forty love.

Eric tries to contain his anger.

ERNIE   *(With contempt)* Yvonne Dinnergong!

Ernie goes to his side of the court.

ERIC   And stop walking like Virginia Wade to try and put me off!

ERNIE   Ready?

ERIC   Yes, I'm …

Ball flashes past Eric. Again he doesn't move. Ernie appears at net; beckons to Eric. Eric goes to net.

ERNIE   First game to me, I think, champ.

ERIC   How am I supposed to play tennis without barley water? Should be barley water here.

ERNIE   You must be worn out the way you've shot around this court. Nevertheless, first set to me.

ERIC   You'll get yours now it's my turn to serve. Machine Gun Morecambe.

ERNIE   Got a good serve then?

ERIC   It'll be so fast the draught from it will whip that right off your head.

ERNIE   I'll risk it.

Ernie goes to his side of the net.

ERIC   Ready for blast-off?

ERNIE   Whenever you like, champ.

ERIC   You won't even see this one, I promise you that.

Eric does a terrible serve: ball goes up and over the hedge.

ERNIE   *(Laughing loudly)* You're right, I didn't see it. Any more good serves like that one champ? Where did you get those shorts: Rent-a-tent?

Eric looks really angry. He serves another terrible one and the ball again goes over hedge.

ERNIE   *(Laughing)* Love fifteen, champ. Keep going. I'll win this game without playing a stroke.

Eric prepares for an almighty serve: he throws the ball up, swings at it, misses it completely. He hurls his racket over the net. Loud cry form Ernie.

ERIC   Out like a light. Game, set and match to me.

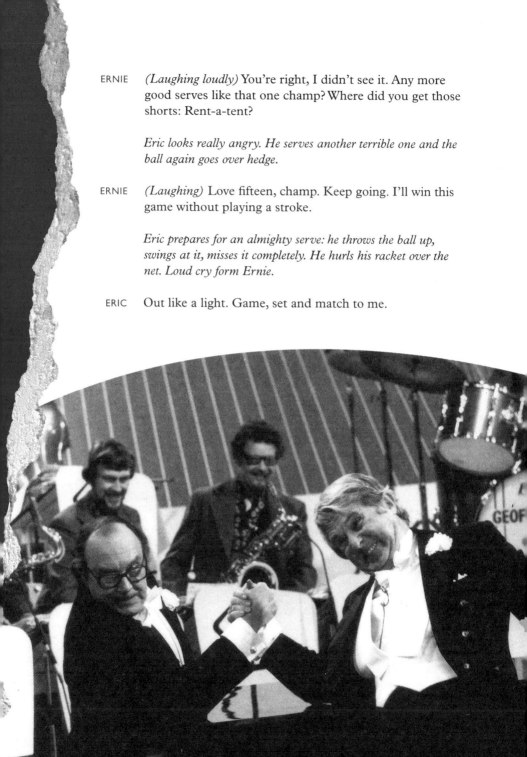

OLD MAN SKETCH

Boys enter: Eric on a walking stick, wearing a white alpaca jacket and a white straw hat. He is made up to appear very old with grey hair sticking out from under the hat.

ERNIE   Good evening ladies and gentlemen – welcome to the show.

ERIC   Tell me what you think.

ERNIE   What do you mean? What do I think?

ERIC   Me! Look at me.

ERNIE   *(Looking)* Smart, just as smart and as well turned out as you are every week.

ERIC   Smart?

ERNIE   As always. Tonight we thought that …

ERIC   No, Ern. That make-up, the grey hair, the wrinkles. I asked them to make me look like a old man.

ERNIE   Do you know I didn't notice the difference. *(Laughs)* I really didn't notice the difference.

ERIC   But they've been nearly four hours making me look like this.

ERNIE   If they'd have waited another month or so they wouldn't have had to bother. *(Laughs)*

Eric looks hurt.

ERIC   I'm supposed to be a very old man not quite in possession of his factories.

ERNIE   Faculties!

ERIC   Just a moment. Can he say faculties? *(Pause)* They're checking up. *(Pause)* No – faculties. Yes, you can.

ERNIE   All right! You want me to ask why you are dressed like an old man?

ERIC   Who?

ERNIE   You.

ERIC   Yes. I have just been offered a character part in a film.

ERNIE   And what am I supposed to do?

ERIC   How many plays have you written?

ERNIE   Oh, Lord knows.

ERIC   That's probably true but he can't have seen every one.

ERNIE   What have my plays got to do with it?

ERIC   You've written lots of character parts and I thought you might be able to give me a few ideas about how to play the part of an old man.

ERNIE   But what about my audience?

ERIC   He rang earlier – he's gone to bingo.

ERNIE   Oh, all right. I'll help you. That's what friends are for. Now show me your old man's walk.

ERIC   Certainly. *(Walks upstage)* Are you ready?

ERNIE   Yes.

ERIC   One old man's walk coming up.

Eric walks briskly downstage.

ERNIE   No idea! You look like Lionel Blair.

ERIC   Well, he is getting on a bit.

ERNIE   Give me that stick and I'll show you.

Ernie walks down as old man.

ERIC   That was marvellous. Now can you talk like an old man, because I find that very difficult.

Ernie walks upstage, then down.

ERNIE   *(Old voice)* Hello, young fellow me lad, I'm an old man.

Eric looks right and left.

ERIC   Keep those sheep out of here.

ERNIE   *(Very proud)* It was me.

ERIC   Good Lord. Do it again!

ERNIE   *(Old voice)* Hello, young fellow me lad, I'm an old man.

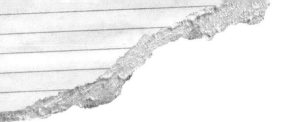

ERIC   Ladies and gentlemen. An Oscar winner on a stick.

ERNIE   Now watch this bit now … *(Knees shaking)* My knees, they're trembling.

ERIC   It's a few years since that happened, but I won't ask you to do the next bit because it's too difficult even for you. Thanks anyway, Ern, let's go now and …

ERNIE   Too difficult for me? Name it.

ERIC   Not even you, Ern.

ERNIE   Name it!

ERIC   Well, in the film this old man, he dies.

ERNIE   That's easy!

He walks upstage.

ERIC   Are you doing it now?

ERNIE   No! *(He staggers for dying act)* Ahh! Doh! Ahhh!

ERIC   *(Watching Ernie)* Good Lord! That is astounding, that is.

Ern makes the most of the dying act, and finishes up on the floor. Gets up and 'dies' again on the floor.

ERIC   Thank you very much, Ern. That's perfect for the film, because it has to be a *very, very* old man.

ERNIE   What's the film called?

ERIC   'The Ernie Wise Story.' *(To camera)* He'll never learn.

DES O' CONNOR JOKE

HAVE YOU GOT ANY PLANS FOR THE FUTURE?

ERIC

I'D LIKE TO DO SOMETHING WITH DES O'CONNOR.

ERNIE

Another couple of picture gags?

Bit of extra dialogue + props.

New Tag.

OPENING SPOT

(ERIC & ERN come thru bets)

ERN: Good evening, ladies and gentlemen, welcome to the show.

ERIC: ~~The voice of the great Ernie Wise.~~

ERN: ~~Thank you.~~

ERIC: ~~A man who has done for British Entertainment what Michael Foot has done for tailoring.~~ (OFFERS TELEGRAM TO ERN) Many Happy Returns of the Day. There's a telegram from the Queen.

ERN: You've actually remembered my birthday?

WHAT ★ THEY ★ WOULDN'T DO TO APPEAR WITH THE COMEDY DUO

THE MORE THAT I think about this next item the more I remember it with some astonishment and a lot of incredulity. I never ever thought that I could get away with this. 'He'll never do that' was the general opinion, and I wasn't surprised. I mean, would you believe that one of the most distinguished and acclaimed actors, a double Oscar winner at that, would agree to walk out on to an empty set, say nothing, not a word for about ten seconds, and then leave? Sir Alec Guinness did. This was his contribution to the 1980 Christmas Show.

> ERIC Are you Mr Wise's taxi? Are you the taxi for Mr Wise?
>
> *Not a movement from Sir Alec.*

 ERIC Would you mind waiting around the back? We are trying to do a show and members of the public aren't allowed out here. Thank you.

Sir Alec turned and walked off to huge applause.

Looking back to some of the truly great stars that we've had on our shows, they have all agreed to do the most outrageous things.

Eric ringing up one of the greatest musicians of all time, Yehudi Menuhin.

Eric wanted to ring Max Jaffa because his name was easier to pronounce, but he rang Yehudi and invited him on to the show, then made a request:

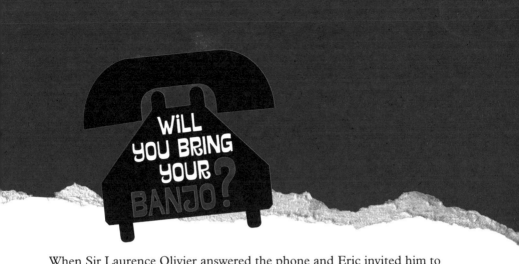

When Sir Laurence Olivier answered the phone and Eric invited him to appear on the show, all wasn't well. Sir Laurence had obviously heard rumours about what happens to guests who appear on that show and he wasn't going to fall for it. What did he do to get out of this corner? Sir Laurence did a Chinese accent.

Other guests got off reasonably lightly. Robin Day had a vase smashed over his head. Flora Robson had a pint of ale poured over her arm and, best of all, Shirley Bassey left wearing a beautiful sequinned dress and a size ten army boot.

My favourite guest put-down? Cliff Richard visiting the flat. Eric handing him a banana with a piece of string tied to it. That was the microphone that Eric gave him to sing his latest release.

How fortunate we were to have the services and the huge talents of all those performers and actors.

Eric is seated on the settee applying the finishing touches with a small paintbrush to a model aeroplane. Ernie enters through main door wearing trendy gear.

ERIC   Hello Ernie.

ERNIE   Hello Eric.

ERIC   What time will you be back?

ERNIE   I've just come in.

ERIC   Been so busy I didn't notice you'd gone.

      Continues painting model.

ERNIE   I've got some wonderful news.

ERIC   You've just lost your tap shoes.

ERNIE   Eric, who would you say is the most popular male singer and entertainer in the country today?

ERIC   *(Too engrossed to be bothered)* Anita Harris.

ERNIE   Now think. 'Bachelor Boy', 'Summer Holiday', 'Livin' Doll'.

ERIC   Give me a clue.

ERNIE   Cliff …

ERIC   Michelmore.

ERNIE   No. Cliff Richard.

ERIC   Oh him.

ERNIE   What do you mean – him? Don't you realise that Cliff wants to come on our show and do a dance routine with us? A dance routine with Cliff Richard.

Ernie gets carried away and starts dance steps. Eric watches.

ERIC   Sit down you silly old fool.

ERNIE   I'm not old. *(He sits)*

ERIC   You do a dance routine with Cliff Richard at your age and you'll make a laughing stock of yourself.

ERNIE   I can still go a bit I can.

ERIC   If your name was 'Dobbin' you'd have been in the knacker's yard ten years ago. And look at you – you've only done half a dozen steps and the sweat's standing out on your forehead.

ERNIE   I'm not sweating.

ERIC   Then the glue must be running.

ERNIE   Then you don't want to do a dance number with Cliff?

ERIC   Where did you meet him?

ERNIE   He was opening that new discotheque down the road.

ERIC   Discotheque? You want to keep away from those places.
        Those Cocoa dancers are too much for you.

ERNIE   Cocoa dancers! Way past it you are!

ERIC   That's right.

ERNIE   Model aeroplanes – about all you can cope with at your age.

ERIC   True.

ERNIE   Well, I'm going to do the dance routine with Cliff. Full of
        youth and vitality I am.

ERIC   Not half. You have to swallow a packet of wheatgerm to
        watch *Top of the Pops*.

ERNIE   Just build your models, Grandad.

        Ernie starts dancing. Doorbell rings.

ERIC   If you've got the strength, answer that.

ERNIE   That'll be Cliff now.

ERIC   Ask him to hang on for a minute while I stitch the sequins on
        to your long johns.

        *Ernie opens door and Cliff enters. Eric carries on painting
        model.*

ERNIE   Cliff, baby!

CLIFF   Hello, Ernie. *(Walks over to Eric)* How are you, Eric?

Cliff takes model from Eric; Eric continues painting nothing.

ERIC   It's taken off. *(Notices Cliff)* Hello – sit down and take the weight off your latest release!

Cliff sits by Eric.

CLIFF   Did you make this, Eric?

ERIC   I'm not really very good at it.

CLIFF   You're kidding. This is beautiful.

ERNIE   I come on first, Cliff. I'll have to wait a minute or two for the applause to stop …

CLIFF   Be with you in just a minute, Ernie. Never seen workmanship like this before.

ERIC   It's a gift. I got the talent from my father. He was an engineer with British Rail – used to weld the crusts on to the meat pies.

CLIFF   And you've always made models?

ERIC   Good Lord, yes. *(Points to Ern)* Made him out of a kit. Trouble is I ran out of wood when I got to his legs.

CLIFF   *(Looks at Ernie)* It's very good – you can't see the join.

ERIC   You're not going to do many of them, are you? I wouldn't like there to be any friction between us.

ERNIE   This is what I had in mind, Cliff.

He puts a record on and we hear 'Livin' Doll'.

ERIC   Take that thing off. You know I can't stand him.

ALL I WANT TO DO AT NIGHT IS PUT ON MY SLIPPERS, LIGHT MY PIPE, BUILD MY MODELS

ERNIE   Cliff's sitting right next to you and you insult one of his records. I'm fed up with you.

CLIFF   What's the matter with Eric?

ERNIE   He's in a bad mood tonight. Ask him why he won't do the dance routine.

CLIFF   Eric, why won't you do the dance routine?

ERIC   Well, all I want to do at night is put on my slippers, light my pipe, build my models …

ERNIE   And watch *Match of the Day*.

ERIC   What? Who said that? I don't want to watch that.

ERNIE   I knew it. *Match of the Day* – it's on tonight. That's why he won't do the dance routine, Cliff.

ERIC   That's got nothing to do with you. I want to finish off this model.

ERNIE   You're like a six-year-old child.

ERIC   *(Picks up model plane and pretends it's in flight and that he is the pilot)* Come in B for Charlie! B for Charlie! 'Bandits' at six o'clock and *The Archers* at a quarter to seven.

ERNIE   Look, Cliff, to do this routine we need three people – will you see if you can get him to do the dance?

CLIFF   Eric, will you do the routine as a special favour – for me?

ERIC   Well, seeing as how you put it like that Cliff – no.

ERNIE   Knew he'd say that.

ERIC   I have got these models to finish.

CLIFF   Eric, if you're only one-tenth as good at dancing as you are at making models, yours could be one of the greatest talents ever seen on the TV screen.

ERIC   Pardon?

ERNIE   *(Quietly to Cliff)* You've got him now.

CLIFF   If you're only one-tenth as good at dancing as you are at making models, yours could be one of the greatest talents ever seen on the TV screen.

ERIC   Well …

CLIFF   Just to satisfy me, would you do a couple of steps now?

ERIC   I don't mind giving you a little treat.

Does a couple of steps and returns to settee.

CLIFF You have no right to keep a talent like that to yourself. That wasn't dancing.

ERIC What do you mean?

CLIFF That was 'leg poetry'.

ERNIE Oh, yes.

CLIFF **YOU MAKE PAN'S PEOPLE LOOK LIKE A GANG OF NAVVIES.**

ERIC There's no answer to that!

CLIFF Your dancing ability has been well fostered – you've obviously been nurtured.

ERIC *(Leans in to Ernie)* Isn't that what they do to tomcats?

CLIFF The world has a right to enjoy your talent.

ERIC *(Gets up)* What are we waiting for, Ern? Cliff and I are waiting to do the routine.

ERNIE Great. Got it all worked out, Cliff. You do the song and Eric and I will do all the movements behind you.

Cliff moves the chair, table and settee.

CLIFF Any particular song?

ERNIE That latest hit you've got – 'Livin' Doll'.

CLIFF Latest hit?

ERNIE You must have heard it – he's never off the radio.

ERIC You know the one.

Eric goes to piano and plays 'Livin' Doll'. Cliff is horrified at the noise. Eric continues; Cliff walks away.

ERNIE   You recognise it?

CLIFF   Oh, yes – it's in there somewhere.

ERIC   Let's rehearse it.

Both take up positions behind Cliff.

ERNIE   Any time you like, Cliff.

CLIFF   Yes. Ready?

Both ready.

Cliff opens his mouth to sing the song and gets only the first couple of words out.

ERNIE   Just a moment!

ERIC   He's gone wrong.

ERNIE   No, he hasn't got a microphone.

Eric gets a banana, with string tied round it for a cable; Eric 'tests' the banana for sound, and gives it to Cliff. Cliff sings 'Livin' Doll' while Eric and Ernie start dancing. Cliff stops singing and watches the boys, looking rather worried.

CLIFF   Boys, I don't know how to say this.

ERIC   Don't say anything.

ERNIE   We know it's good.

CLIFF   Yes, it's … but don't you think … what you're doing is a little old-fashioned??

Long, horrified pause.

CLIFF   What I mean is … I'm singing a sort of new type of song and your routine is very old.

Another long pause.

CLIFF   I mean … in any case, I saw you do the same thing with Tom Jones.

BOTH   Who?

CLIFF   Tom Jones.

ERNIE   Oh, that six-footer, curly hair, well set up.

ERIC   Thought that was Nina.

CLIFF   Can we do one of Ernie's plays?

ERNIE   No.

Moves right with disgust.

ERIC   You've offended him now.

CLIFF   I was thinking of something a bit more 'with it' – like this.

Cliff dances.

ERIC   We don't want to get laughs!

ERNIE   Three American sailors on board a battleship doing a dance routine with mops.

ERIC   Never been done before.

CLIFF   Never been done before! But didn't I see Gene Kelly do that in a film?

ERNIE   Never.

ERIC   Gene Kelly. She'd never dress up as an American sailor.

ERNIE   Not now that she's Princess Grace of Meccano.

CLIFF: I didn't realise.

ERIC   Be guided by us.

CLIFF   Well all right then, we'll do it your way. But are you sure it's going to work?

Eric takes the banana from him and eats it.

ERIC   If you're really worried we'll get that singing group at the back of you – Olivier, Newton and John. Three nice fellows.

FREUD MIGHT HAVE HAD THOUGHTS ABOUT THESE LINES

ERNIE I've extended my repertoire.
ERIC It doesn't show from back here.

ERNIE He wanted to expose her feminine folly.
ERIC He can't do that – there's frost about.

ERNIE My auntie's got a whistler.
ERIC Now there's a novelty.

These couple of lines were taken from a Casanova sketch.

ERNIE   I think I've curried her favours.

ERIC   You've very nearly casseroled her dumplings.

Interior, bedroom. Ernie is in bed, writing. Eric is standing, looking out of the window. A police siren is heard speeding past.

Eric: He's not going to sell much ice cream going at that speed.

ERNIE'S *Literary* PROJECT

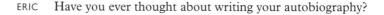

ERIC   Have you ever thought about writing your autobiography?

ERNIE   The story of my life?

ERIC   You could do both.

ERNIE   My autobiography and the story of my life?

ERIC   I don't see why not. You're very gifted, you could do both. You've got that new ballpoint.

ERNIE   That's true. Yes. Yes, I could do it. I had a very interesting childhood.

ERIC   It still is.

ERNIE   When I was born I came as a complete surprise to my mother.

ERIC   She was expecting a roll of lino.

ERNIE   That's a very old joke.

ERIC   If you can remember it, it must be ancient.

ERNIE   I'm not sure about this idea. I'll have to give it some thought.

ERIC   Your humble little home with the rather quaint name, 'Condemned'.

ERNIE   I said I'd think about it.

ERIC   You owe your public. He's very loyal, he'd buy a copy.

ERNIE   I said I'll think about it. I'll have a ponder.

LITERARY Talk

Ernie: What are you reading?

Eric: Charles Dickens.

Ernie: Who's it by?

Eric: Oliver Twist.

Ernie: Have you joined the library?

Eric: I failed the medical.

Ernie: Who's your favourite author?

Eric: Askey.

BYRON MEETS KEATS

(RE-WRITE)

```
            TAKES PLACE IN A TEASHOP OF 1880's
            ERN AS LORD BYRON IS SEATED AT A TABLE.
            ERIC AS KEATS IS STANDING BY THE TABLE TALKING TO THE WAITRESS.
            ERN SEES HIM AND RISES.

ERN.        My dear Keats'
ERIC.       Lord Byron.
ERN.        Two poets meet
ERIC.       How do you do.
ERN.        My dear chap, please take a pew.
            BOTH SIT OPPOSITE SIDES OF THE TABLE. WAITRESS NOT FAR AWAY.
ERIC.       I've been abroad.
ERN.        Nobody said. Nice or Cannes?
ERIC.       No, Birkenhead.
ERN.        Are you still seeing the baker's lass, Elsie McGovern?
ERIC.       Not anymore.
ERN.        Why?
ERIC.       She's got one in the oven.
ERN.        A young maid in a bakehouse, not the best of jobs.
ERIC.       But you should have seen the queue for her crusty cobs. And what of
            your wife?
ERN.        I'm trying to dodger.
ERIC.       You don't mean ..
ERN.        Yes.
```

ERN.   Yes.

ERIC.   I never trusted that lodger. I've written a poem

ERN.   Oh, joy' What a thrill'

ERIC.   It was for me, I sat on the quill.

ERN.   Does your poem have a title?

ERIC.   The Wayward Rover.

GIRL.   What would you like?

ERIC.   How about a turnover?

GIRL.   (TO ERN) How about you sir, something now on the table?

ERIC.   He's tired, his back's gone and I don't think he's able.

ERN.   How are your dumplings?

ERIC.   They look fine to me.

ERN.   I'll have two of those and a nice cup of tea.
        WAITRESS EXITS.

ERN.   I'm wild about dumplings, I think that they're great.

ERIC.   She'll have a hell of a job getting them onto a plate. Can you
        write a poem?

ERN.   A poem? You bet' I'll write one now on this serviette (WRITES AND
        SPEAKS ALOUD) I am a poet, I make things rhyme, I find that I'm
        doing it all the time. 0've written of flowers, of birds and birds
        but never about a Scotsman with housemaids knees.

ERIC.   My dear chap, I don't know how you do it' Well done' Bravo' You've
        won a cruet' (PASSES ERN THE SALT) Now let me see what I can do.
        I think I can write one better than you (WRITING AND SPEAKING ALOUD)
        Lord Byron you're so debonair, around you people flock, the way
        they did last Saturday night when you wore your Auntie's frock.

ERN.   (RISES IN ANGER) How dare you write of me like that' I refuse to
        stand for this'

ERIC.   I know it's true and so do you' Shut up and give us a kiss'
        ERN EXITS AS WAITRESS ENTERS.

ERIC.   You're a bonny wench from what I can see, and what I can see is
        good.

HIRL.   Do you think you could write a poem about me?

ERIC.   Sweet thing, I'm sure I could. I'll write a poem about your name,
        my poem will bring you lasting fame.

GIRL.   Then I'll tell you my name, it's Norah Pitts.

ERIC.   Could I have the bill, please?

THE PLAY WHAT ERN *wrote*

T
O SEE MORECAMBE without Wise would be like looking at Blackpool without the Tower. No Eric and Ern 'Best Of' would be acceptable, certainly not to me, without a flat sketch and Ern writing yet another play. The two of them trapped in the flat will forever be my favourite Morecambe and Wise situation. We join them with Ern tapping two-fingered at the typewriter.

ERIC   Another masterpiece?

ERNIE   I suppose so. This is the most difficult play I have ever written, it's taken me almost twenty minutes.

ERIC   Have you ever thought about writing a full-length epic for the screen?

ERNIE   Tomorrow.

ERIC   I'm sure you will. The talent was always there, even as a lad. Remember that composition you wrote at school?

ERNIE   It was all about 'My Pet'. The poodle we used to have at home.

ERIC   Sad, that was. I cried when Miss read it to us.

ERNIE   It was very sad.

ERIC   The way it died after biting your Auntie May. How many awards have you won this year?

ERNIE   Thirty-seven.

ERIC   Including Crufts? Ern, I think that the time has come for you to accept a challenge.

AN
ABC THEATRE
PROGRAMME

THE
MORECAMBE
& WISE
SHOW

ERNIE   A challenge?

ERIC   Write a musical play, there's money in it. Just look at how well Agatha Mitchell has done out of *The Black And White Mousetrap*.

ERNIE   That's been running for twenty years.

ERIC   They got through two hundred and forty-two usherettes.

ERNIE   Do you think I could write musical play?

ERIC   You, Ern, could become another Lionel Burke.

ERNIE   Bart.

ERIC   Has he? I didn't know that. Look what *The Sound of Music* did for Eamonn Andrews.

ERNIE   Julie Andrews.

ERIC   You know him better than I do. *Showboat*. That was a great musical. Who could ever forget Dame Flora Robson standing on that bale of hay and singing 'Old Man River'? Write a musical this afternoon about Lew Grade: *Promises Promises*.

ERNIE   It's been done.

ERIC   Not by him it hasn't.

ERNIE   Write a musical? I'm sure I could do it. Eric, are you looking at something interesting out of that window?

ERIC   I'm just a simple fellow.

ERNIE   That's true.

ERIC   But to me that is the most beautiful sight that any man could

ERNIE What is?

ERIC Ada Bailey hanging out her knickers on the clothes line.

ERNIE Come away from that window.

Telephone ringing, Ern lifts the receiver.

ERNIE Hello, Ernie Wise here … You're a fellow writer? Gosh!! I'm
a fellow writer as well … I'm going to write a musical this
afternoon, if it doesn't rain. You live in the same block of
flats? So do I. Why don't you come over for a little chat? …
Splendid, look forward to meeting you.

ERIC Fellow writer?

ERNIE Lives in the same block of flats.

ERIC So do you.

ERNIE I told him that. He's coming over to meet me. He's a poet.

ERIC I used to fancy myself as a poet.

ERNIE You write poetry? You couldn't leave a note for the milkman.

ERIC Monologues. I do a lot of those. There used to be a fellow on
the musical halls years ago named Tony Bennett. 'Almost
a Gentleman'.

ERNIE Billie Bennett.

ERIC Could you wish for anything more poetic than this? Just
listen to how this scans;

Digging for grapes with a bicycle lamp,
By the light of a lantern jaw …

Eric is interrupted by the doorbell ringing.

ERIC The bell's just gone. Don't stand there, there's
somebody at the door.

ERNIE	Rubbish that is. Answer the door.

Eric opens the door. A very effeminate man enters.

MAN	Hello to you, old fellow.
ERIC	Can I help you, Miss?
ERNIE	You're the fellow who lives across the way, you called a few minutes ago.
MAN	Yes. I thought I'd give you a ring.
ERIC	I hope you'll both be very happy together.
ERNIE	My name's Ernie Wise, playwriter. Please sit down.
ERIC	Take the weight off your mascara.
ERNIE	I didn't quite get your name.
MAN	Adrian, Adrian Fondle.
ERIC	Sounds like a new bra.
MAN	That's my pen name. My real name is Adrian Caress.
ERNIE	Do tell about the poems what you're writing, Adrian.
MAN	Well …
ERIC	I do a bit of poetry writing.
MAN	Really. How so terribly fascinating.
ERIC	I've just finished one called 'The Fairy'. Nothing personal. My forte is monologues. I've got forty monologues in the next room.

THERE'S A HELL OF A SMELL IN DINGLEY DELL, THE FAIRIES ARE WASHING THEIR SOCKS, WHEN UP JUMPS A SAILOR ...

ERNIE Why don't you shut up! Spoil everything you do! I'm so sorry about this, Mr ...

MAN Call me Adrian.

ERNIE Call me Ern.

ERIC Call me tomorrow. I've had enough of this.

ONE FROM THE TOMBS

TUTANKHAMUN SKETCH

ERNIE HAVE YOU GOT THE SCROLLS?

ERIC NO. IT'S THESE SHORTS THEY'VE JUST COME BACK FROM THE CLEANERS.

GUESS WHAT?

OVER THE YEARS I have countless times, particularly when I'm lost for ideas, which is like every day, just put down two opening lines, as above, completely clueless as to where they were going or what the subject of the routine was going to be.

I'd sit and look at those two lines, pace around the room trying to think what Ern would never guess.

That Eric has a girl? He's going on holiday alone? He's been arrested for shoplifting? He's thinking of growing a beard?

It has worked in the past – not very often – but it has worked.

All the little tricks we use in our desperate, sometimes frantic quest for laughs.

I have on the wall in front of my desk a twelve-inch square which I drew with a ballpoint. It's to represent a blank TV screen and I often just stare at it and wait for it to spring to life and inspire me. It did work, and I remember it memorably because it led to some of my favourite sketches – Oggy, the ten-foot ventriloquist doll, was one of them.

But what about the opening lines? Well, this is what happened.

Eric: Ern, you'll never guess.

Ernie: Tell me. Tell me what I'll never guess.

Eric: I've been asked to do a commercial for TV.

Ernie: You!

Eric: Yes.

Ernie: For dog food? Do you have to lie in a bowl?

Eric: You can mock. I have been invited.

Ernie: Invited.

Eric: Yes. I have been invited to make a TV commercial for
       an insurance company.

Ernie: Don't make me laugh! You can't write and you know
       nothing about insurance.

Eric: Do you want to hear my commercial?

Ernie: This'll be good. Go on.

Eric: Have you had a accident at work that wasn't your fault
       and it's resulted in your death? Then ring this number
       now!

Ernie: That is the most ridiculous commercial I have ever
       heard!

Eric: Oh! They'll be ringing up in their thousands after
       that commercial goes out, sunshine.

VANESSA REDGRAVE

ERNIE My famous play about Napoleon next.

ERIC With Vanessa Redcoat?

ERNIE Redgrave. She gave us a few problems.

ERIC With her being such a tall girl?

ERNIE Do you know she wanted paying by the inch.

ERIC We'd have been skint. A delightful lady to work with.

ERNIE   Affable.

ERIC   Always thought she was British.

ERNIE   She worked hard at rehearsal.

ERIC   Did you see her during the breaks? She was stretched out fast asleep in three separate dressing rooms.

ERNIE   Vanessa rather liked me.

ERIC   Oh?

ERNIE   Offered me a lift home in her car.

ERIC   Fool!

ERNIE   What do you mean?

ERIC   It was only because she didn't have a dipstick.

ERNIE   This is a play of mine we did in one of our Christmas shows with Vanessa Redgrave.

ERIC   We wanted a big bird for Christmas and we got one.

ERNIE   I think you should go and get ready to appear in my play, Miss Vanessa.

VANESSA   Of course. I'll be right back.

ERIC   You're big enough to play in goal.

Napoleon & Josephine

WITH

VANESSA REDGRAVE

NAPLEON: Ernie Wise
JOSEPHINE: Vanessa Redgrave
WELLINGTON: Eric Morcambe

Scene: In the richly furnished tent used by Napoleon on the battlefield of Waterloo. Tent is deserted. F/X heavy gunfire and the distant shouting of men in battle. Ernie enters as Napoleon; staggers around the tent before standing still and looking very distressed.

ERNIE   Sacre Beaujolais! That it should come to this – that I, Napoleon Bonaparte, the tenacious Corsican, should come to this. Defeated by that devil, Wellington. Sacre Beaujolais and bon appetit.

Ernie bows his head and is sobbing … as Vanessa Redgrave enters as Josephine, looking seductive. She stops and sees Ernie sobbing.

VANESSA   He is crying again. I wish he wouldn't cry. The tears roll down his legs and make them shrink. I do love him. When he kisses me I can feel his heart beating against my kneecaps.

She crosses to Ernie and places an arm on his shoulder.

VANESSA   Napoleon, sit down.

ERNIE   I am sat down.

VANESSA   Napoleon, my beloved, tell your Josephine what has happened.

ERNIE   The flower of the French Army lies crushed upon the battlefield of Waterloo. I have lost some of my finest men.

VANESSA   What about the big red-headed drummer lad?

ERNIE   What?

VANESSA   The one with the big cymbals.

ERNIE   Oh him. Gone. Your Napoleon has been defeated.

VANESSA   You must have known in your heart that defeat was inevitable.

ERNIE   I must be honest, two nights ago I had a slight inkling.

VANESSA   Why didn't you tell me? I was awake. I take it that you have lost to the Duke of Wellington.

ERNIE   He is at this very moment on his way here with the terms of the surrender.

Sounds of horses' hooves. Eric enters as Wellington. Hooves continue.

ERIC   That horse never stops … Evenin' all. Sorry I'm late. Some fool kept me talking. Said he wanted to name a rubber boot after me. The Duke of Wellington at your service.

Eric salutes. Ernie salutes; pulls rabbit out of jacket.

ERNIE   Napoleon Bonaparte.

ERIC   *(Walks past Vanessa to Ernie)* I don't want to worry you but this tent pole's loose.

ERNIE   How dare you, sir. That tent pole is the Empress Josephine.

Ernie places a small box in front of Vanessa. He stands on it and faces her.

ERNIE   Tell him who you are.

VANESSA   I am indeed the Empress Josephine of France.

ERIC   And what are you doing up at the front? Not that it matters – it suits you.

VANESSA   The Emperor wishes to discuss the Battle of Waterloo.

ERIC   Odd name for a battle. There was no water and I couldn't find a …

ERNIE   *(Getting off box)* How dare you!

VANESSA   Boney, my darling.

ERNIE   Not tonight, Josephine.

ERIC   What does he mean?

ERNIE   It is of little consequence.

VANESSA   *(Looking at Eric)* I'll second that.

ERIC   *(To standard)* What do you think of it so far? *(Vents)* 'Ruggish'.

ERNIE   Now let us sit down and discuss these terms properly.

VANESSA   I'll take everything down.

ERIC   That'll get a few laughs.

Vanessa and Eric sit down.

VANESSA   Have you got the scrolls?

ERIC   No, I always walk like this.

ERNIE   The meeting is now in session.

He bangs the table with a mallet; hits Eric's finger.

ERIC   Ow!

VANESSA   *(Reads paper)* These terms are a bit one-sided.

ERNIE   I'll say they are. Are you prepared to ratify *my* proposals?

ERIC   Certainly. Put them on the table and pass me that mallet.

VANESSA   You want everything your own way.

ERIC   Oh, you've heard!

ERNIE   We are having no part of this document.

VANESSA   What happens when Napoleon signs these surrender terms?

ERIC   He will be dragged out by the dragoons. Not a pretty sight! *(To Vanessa)* I wouldn't look if I were you.

VANESSA   I've never heard anything so terrible.

ERIC   Oh you must have done! Have you heard Max Bygraves singing 'Deck of Cards' – that takes a bit of beating.

ERNIE   Perfectly true, Duke.

ERIC   Anyway, you will be taken to St Helena and incarcerated.

VANESSA   That'll bring tears to his eyes.

ERIC   *(To camera)* They're all at it.

ERNIE   I think I should have a word with you, Josephine. *(Stands)* Over here. *(Points, and pulls rabbit out)*

Vanessa and Ernie move to one side. Eric moves behind them and listens.

ERNIE   We've got to find a way out of this.

VANESSA   He's such a stubborn man.

ERNIE   It's not going to be easy.

VANESSA   We could offer him money.

ERNIE   I've got an idea.

VANESSA   What's that?

ERIC   Seduce him.

VANESSA   *(To Ernie)* Do you think I could?

ERIC   Yes, he'd love it.

ERNIE   That's a good idea.

Ernie turns to Eric.

ERNIE   My Lord Duke …

ERIC   Oh there you are. I didn't understand a word because you were talking in French. Are you talking in French now?

ERNIE   No, I'm not … I need time to study these terms.

VANESSA   *(Aside to Ernie)* Just give me five minutes alone with him.

ERIC   That's no good. It takes me twenty minutes to get my wellies off.

ERNIE   I shall be in the anteroom. *(Exits)*

VANESSA We are alone.

ERIC   Ready when you are, pally.

VANESSA Poor Napoleon, he's been going through a bad time. Since his retreat from Moscow, he's been very cold towards me.

ERIC   Well, with that deep snow and those short legs … say no more. *(Nudges Vanessa)* Would um … *(Moves centre, to bed)* … would you like something to warm you up?

VANESSA I would very much.

ERIC   Good. I think I've got some extra-strong mints in my greatcoat.

VANESSA I think no. Wellie … ?

ERIC   Yes.

VANESSA Napoleon has been so engrossed in the battle that he's tended to neglect me.

ERIC   Oh.

VANESSA I am a woman.

ERIC   Have you told him?

VANESSA I like you. *(She sprays perfume on to her neck)* 'Midnight in Paris'.

ERIC   *(Picks up bottle and dabs his cheeks with it)* Two fifteen in Darlington – just before the kick-off.

         Vanessa indicates that Eric should sit on the sofa.

VANESSA Please?

ERIC   Do you want to sell it?

VANESSA Sit by me. I only wish we had some music.

ERIC   That's easily arranged.

         Picks up hat; it turns into accordion.

VANESSA I am beginning to like you very much. I wish we could have met in Paris. It's a beautiful city. Put the candle out.

ERIC   Where's the switch?

VANESSA Blow it out and we can make love.

ERIC   Yes. *(Attempts to blow candle out, but it lights each time)* By the time I blow this thing out, I'll be too tired to make love.

VANESSA Never mind the candle. *(She cuddles up to Eric)* The better the light, the better the love.

ERIC   It's no use, I've just had a power cut.

VANESSA I think I'm falling in love with you.

ERIC   I have a wife in England.

VANESSA It's common knowledge that your wife has another.

ERIC   Now there's a novelty.

VANESSA Kiss me!

         Vanessa throws her arms about Eric. A very long kiss. Eric shudders and bangs his legs.

ERIC   Good lord. Have you got shares in Mothercare?

VANESSA I don't know what it is you're doing to me, but I can feel a pounding in my bosom.

ERIC   Have a look, it might be one of his rabbits.

VANESSA   *(Sits up)* So you think you can resist me?

Eric lunges and misses.

ERIC   Oh yes.

VANESSA   Really?

She raises her skirt and reveals a Luton Town rosette below her knee.

ERIC   I've got news for you: we're going up the League.

Eric and Vanessa embrace and lean back. Ernie enters.

ERNIE   Sacre Beaujolais and bon appetit! What is going on?

Vanessa and Eric quickly rise.

VANESSA   Napoleon!

ERIC   Don't jump to conclusions. I can explain everything. I was carrying on with your wife behind your back.

ERNIE   This is too much.

Takes hand from tunic and brings out rabbit.

ERIC   Have you got Harry Corbett in there passing them to you?

ERNIE   First I lose the battle. Now I have lost my wife.

VANESSA   That's not true.

ERNIE   I love you so much, Josephine. You must choose between me or him.

ERIC   *(Pulls his hand out – no rabbit)* Yes, you must choose between me or him. And, remember, this is the book of the play and we can't finish with a song.

VANESSA   What a shame, because I thought I sang so well.

ERIC   I couldn't hear you. You were too high up.

ERNIE   Josephine, the time has come for you to choose.

ERIC   I know we finished the sketch with a song on the telly, but this is a book so think of a new tag or we're all in trouble.

VANESSA   Very well.

ERNIE   You have made your choice, Josephine?

VANESSA   I have.

ERNIE   Is it me?

VANESSA   No.

ERIC   Then it is me!

VANESSA   No.

ERIC   If it's not me …

ERNIE   And it's not me …

VANESSA   It is Christmas and with the money you're paying me I won't have a decent dinner so I'll take the rabbit.

She reaches inside Eric's tunic and takes the rabbit.

ERIC   Don't go. I've got twelve more rabbits hidden away in there if you'd care to get them out.

VANESSA   Gladly.

She puts her hand inside Eric's tunic.

ERIC   Oh yes! Keep going …

THAT PIANO CONCERTO

STILL BEING REPEATED more than forty years on, Eric and Ernie's Grieg Piano Concerto is said by many to have been the greatest of all their comedy routines.

The contribution made by André Previn was quite unforgettable. How producer John Ammonds ever got Andre to do the show astonished all three of us. André Previn, the most famous musician in the world and he'd agreed to come on the show? When John told me I knew that I had to write something extra special.

To answer the question I have been asked SO many times: 'Who was your favourite guest out of almost one hundred shows'? it has to be André Previn.

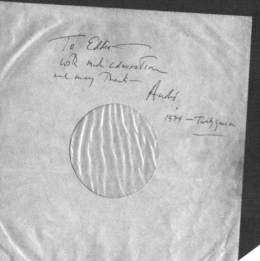

I loved Glenda, Dame Flora, Peter, Cilla Black, Shirley Bassey and Cliff Richard. The list goes on. But none of them could play the jazz piano like André. His album and version of *My Fair Lady* for me is one of the greatest jazz piano discs ever.

Delighted as Eric, Ernie and myself were at the prospect of having André on the show, we were very

THE RECORD SLEEVE WHAT ANDRÉ SIGNED

apprehensive. Would a classical music magician be able to cope with our basic music hall comedy?

There was a golden moment in the show in the dialogue in front of the curtains when he proves most definitely that he could.

André agreed to conduct the piece:

ANDRÉ **Well … All right. I'll get my baton.**

ERNIE **Please do that.**

ANDRÉ **It's in Chicago.**

The timing of that line was immaculate. Just the very slightest pause, a pause that came so naturally to him, 'It's in Chicago'. That's what did it. The man was multi-talented.

The relief on Eric's face is so obvious, watch for it next time it's replayed.

After that magical moment the rest of the sketch was a joy.

Shortly before we began recording that sketch, I went to André's dressing room with my copy of his *My Fair Lady* album. He signed it for me. We chatted for a few minutes and I didn't see what he'd written inside the cover until I returned home to Liverpool the following day.

He'd written: 'To Eddie with much admiration, André Previn.'

I treasure that album. Even all these years on it still makes me feel so very proud. 'With much admiration'. I still can't believe that.

THE GRIEG
Piano Concerto BY
GRIEG

ERNIE Now one of the highlights of the evening, a truly great international star ... Good evening ... And now we have another famous person from the world of music. Let's give a warm welcome to the principal conductor of the London Symphony Orchestra, Mr André Previn!

André Previn enters from behind the curtain.

ERNIE Thank you for bringing your many musical talents to our humble little show.

ANDRÉ Well, thank you for that tremendous introduction. It doesn't come out of my fee, does it?

ERNIE Fee? What fee? Oh, a joke ... I suppose you're looking forward to tonight?

ANDRÉ Well now, who wouldn't? I've come a long way to conduct the Mendelssohn Violin Concerto, especially with Yehudi Menuhin as my soloist.

ERNIE Yes ...

ANDRÉ I'll tell the truth, I wasn't going to come on your show at all 'till you told me that Yehudi Menuhin had agreed to play.

ERNIE I did say that, did I?

ANDRÉ Yes. By the way, has Yehudi arrived yet?

ERNIE Who?

ANDRÉ Yehudi Menuhin.

ERNIE   I'm glad you asked that. As a matter of fact I can explain the whole situation; it won't take a minute …

A hand appears from behind the curtain holding a piece of paper.

ERNIE   Well, what do you know! It's a telegram. *(Smacks the hand which has turned palm up as if asking for a tip)* Oh dearie me, it's from Yehudi.

ANDRÉ   Who?

ERNIE   Yehudi Menuhin.

ANDRÉ   Of course. What does he say?

ERNIE   Oh, he says he can't come. He says 'Dear boys, I can't make it on your show, opening at the Argyle Theatre, Birkenhead in *Old King Cole*'. What a shame, a shame.

ANDRÉ   Yes. *(Takes telegram and reads it)* Good night. *(Turns to leave)*

ERNIE   No, please don't go. There are other great musicians and other great works.

ANDRÉ   Such as?

ERNIE   Such as Grieg's Piano Concerto.

ANDRÉ   You're right, that's a great work. But do you have someone of the calibre of Mr Menuhin?

ERNIE   Who?

ANDRÉ   Yehudi Menuhin.

ERNIE   Oh yes. Better.

ANDRÉ   You have someone better than Yehudi Menuhin?

ERNIE   Yes. Can knock spots off him. I think that you're in for the thrill of a lifetime. Ladies and gentlemen, here to play Grieg's Piano Concerto: Mr Eric Morecambe.

Eric enters wearing full evening tails.

ERIC   *(To Ern)* It's fixed.

ERNIE   *(To Eric)* It's fixed.

ERIC   Mr Preview, it's a pleasure to meet you, and ready when you are – a-one-a-two, a-one-two-three-four …

ANDRÉ   *(To Ernie)* You got me here under false pretences.

ERIC   False pretences? What's he mean?

ERNIE   I told you it wouldn't work, he's expecting Yehudi Menuhin.

ANDRÉ   He's a comedian.

ERIC   And a very funny one, too. I must be honest, he makes me laugh when he puts the violin under his chin, gets to the last bar and shouts, 'Aye aye, that's yer lot!' and goes straight to the bar. I'm very keen on him.

ANDRÉ   Eric Morecambe is a comedian, he can't play the piano.

ERIC   Just a moment sir, you seem to doubt my musical prowess.

ANDRÉ   I certainly do.

ERIC   Now let me put your mind at rest, sir, because you are now looking at one of the few men to have fished off the end of Sir Henry Wood's Promenade. Now follow that with sea lions!

ERNIE   I was there when he did it.

ERIC   Of course you were, you put the bait on.

ANDRÉ   Good night, gentlemen. *(Turns to leave; Eric and Ern stop him)*

ERIC   Don't go please.

ANDRÉ   I don't dispute for one moment that Mr Morecambe is a great comic, I just find it difficult to believe that he can play Grieg's Piano Concerto.

ERIC   Tell him.

ERNIE   I do assure you that he knows it. I assure you, Mr Preview.

ERIC   Privett!

ANDRÉ   Previn!

ERNIE   He knows all the masterpieces – The Planets suite by Gustav Holst.

ERIC   Not forgetting the three-piece suite by Arthur Negus. Who was it, do you think – look at me when I'm talking to you … oh you are – who was it, do you think introduced Glenda Jackson to Tchaikovsky?

ANDRÉ   I don't know.

ERIC   Me! *(To Ern)* Wasn't it?

ERNIE   Yes.

ERIC   And if you don't believe me you can get in contact with the other world-famous conductor, Sir Ivy Bennett. He'll tell you all about me.

ERNIE He certainly will.

ANDRÉ Good night. *(Turns to leave)*

ERNIE Don't go Mr Preview!

ERIC Privett!

ANDRÉ Previn!

ERNIE I can assure you that he is more than capable.

ANDRÉ Well, alright, I'll get my baton.

ERNIE Please do.

ANDRÉ It's in Chicago.

ERIC 'It's in Chicago!' Ha ha. Pow! I like him!

ERNIE We've got one here. Believe me, you're in for a surprise Mr Preview.

ERIC Previn!

ANDRÉ Privett!

ERNIE Open the curtains please.

Behind the curtains an orchestra is 'tuning up'. A rostrum with music stand is in the centre, a black grand piano to the left of the rostrum. André, Eric and Ern mount the rostrum.

ERIC Is this the band?

ERNIE This is the band, yes.

ERIC Seen better bands on a cigar. Which one's the fixer?

ERNIE The one in the gold lamé suit.

ERIC They usually are. Right, I'll go get the music.

*Eric meanders to the piano, going up and down three steps to
the front and to the side of the rostrum. He stops with one hand
on the piano's open lid.*

ERIC Incidentally, where's the piano? Never mind, this will do.
*(Takes some sheet music out of the piano and shows it to
André)* I hope you understand these squiggles?

ANDRÉ I do.

ERIC The reason I ask, is because the second movement is
particularly interesting to me. You see, in the second
movement I don't like hearing the banjos too loud.

ANDRÉ Oh, no.

ERIC Keep it down. None of that 'uchnga-uchanga'; that's vulgar.

ANDRÉ We'll keep it way down.

ERIC That's the phrase I was looking for: 'way down'. That's me
there, you see? *(He holds the sheet music to the camera; it has
a photo of Eric seated at a piano, one arm raised high above
the keyboard)* Me playing the Grieg Piano Concerto. *(He
shows it to the orchestra)* A signed copy after the show, lads.

ERNIE Now, if I could just explain to Mr Preview, I would like you
to notice that Eric plays the original version.

ERIC The one we played before we went decimal.

ANDRÉ Wait though, this isn't the original version. I'll explain; after
the opening timpani roll in the original, the piano takes
over, but you've got that played by the whole orchestra.

ERIC   *(Raises his glasses and peers at the sheet music)* Oh yes, but this is a special version.

ANDRÉ   A special arrangement of the Grieg Piano Concerto? I've never heard of that before.

ERIC   That's the idea. Everybody plays it the old way. I thought we'd do something different.

ANDRÉ   Alright, whatever you say.

ERNIE   I'll announce it then, shall I?

ANDRÉ   Yes, please do.

ERIC   *(To André)* You're doing well, son, doing well.

ERNIE   Ladies and gentlemen, tonight Grieg's Piano Concerto by Grieg, soloist Mr Eric Morecambe, conducted by Mr André Previn.

The music begins with the orchestral introduction. As it plays Eric meanders to the piano, going up and down the steps of the rostrum. Just as he gets to the keyboard, his cue is missed. He stands at the side of the piano with his hands outstretched.

ANDRÉ   What's the matter?

Eric and Ern stride onto the rostrum together.

ERIC   You see, the introduction …

ANDRÉ   What's wrong with it?

ERIC   It's too short.

ANDRÉ   It's too short?

ERIC   Oh, you noticed?

ANDRÉ   Yes. By how much is it too short?

ERIC Well, I went down here like this. *(Begins the same meander to the piano from the rostrum)*

ANDRÉ You wasted some time there.

ERIC Yes, but I was here, *(stands at the side of the keyboard)* and it's about ... *(he stretches one leg back toward the rostrum)* this much too short.

ANDRÉ That much. *(André stands with his arms wide apart, measuring)*

ERNIE About a yard.

ERIC If you could lengthen it by about a yard, we'll be in.

ANDRÉ What do you think we could do about that?

ERIC It's nothing to do with me. I let my musical manager handle things like that. *(Looks to Ern)*

ERNIE Could we get in touch with Grieg?

ERIC That's a good idea.

ANDRÉ You mean call him on the phone?

ERNIE We could call him on the phone, why not?

ANDRÉ I didn't bring his number with me.

ERIC Well it's Norway something or other, isn't it?

ERNIE What's the code?

ERIC Fingal's Cave, isn't it? Mind you, he might not be in, might be out skiing.

ANDRÉ Could we just start again, do you think?

ERIC I tell you what, this time I'll sit down waiting.

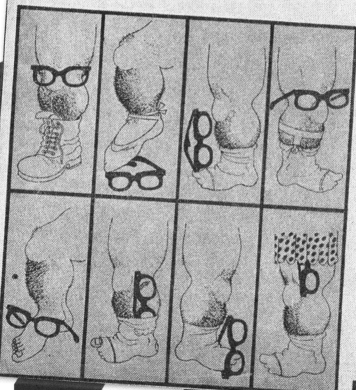

ANDRÉ   What a good idea, you'll be ready!

Eric goes to piano.

ERNIE   I'll introduce it again, shall I? Ladies and gentlemen, Grieg's Piano Concerto, soloist Eric Morecambe, conductor Andrew Preview.

Opening bars play, Eric waits at the keyboard. When his cue comes he can't see André because of the piano lid, and so misses it.

ANDRÉ   Any time you're ready …

ERIC   Can I have a word with you please? *(André goes to the piano, the pair attempt to see each other over and under the piano lid; finally André leans under the lid)* The point is, I hope you don't mind me saying this, but when you got to the part that was my cue, I couldn't see you because of the piano lid.

ANDRÉ   I don't know what I can do.

YOU'RE PLAYING ALL THE WRONG NOTES!

I'M PLAYING ALL THE RIGHT NOTES. BUT NOT NECESSARILY IN THE RIGHT ORDER.

ERIC   Was it? Yes. In the way.

ANDRÉ   I don't know what we can do about that.

ERNIE   He wants to be taller. *(To André)* Could you wear high heels?

ANDRÉ   Again?

ERIC   You don't have to.

ANDRÉ   I don't know what I can do.

ERIC   I have a suggestion. Would you jump in the air so I can see you over the lid of the piano?

ANDRÉ   You want me to jump in the air on the rostrum so you can see my cue.

ERIC   Yes, if you could do that for me.

ANDRÉ   Yes, I'll do that for you. *(He returns to the rostrum)*

ERNIE   I'll announce it again. Ladies and gentlemen, Grieg, by him and him.

The opening bars sound and when Eric's cue comes, André leaps in the air and points toward Eric, who stands.

ERIC   Great!

He proceeds to play a vamp that bears no resemblance to Grieg's Piano Concerto. Ern dances beside him. André stands wide-eyed with disbelief before marching down to the keyboard, leaning on the piano and staring at Eric, who slowly stops playing.

ERIC   Something wrong with the violins?

ANDRÉ   No, there's nothing wrong with the violins.

ERIC   That's just your opinion.

ANDRÉ   What were you playing just then?

ERIC   The Grieg Piano Concerto. *(Resumes his vamp)*

ANDRÉ   *(Stopping him)* But you're playing all the wrong notes!

Eric rises, steps over to André and pulls him close by his lapels.

ERIC   I'm playing all the right notes. But not necessarily in the right order. I give you that, sunshine. *(He slaps André's cheeks)*

ERNIE   That sounded quite reasonable to me. Are you satisfied, Mr Preview?

ANDRÉ   No.

ERIC   What do you mean, 'No'?

ANDRÉ   With all due deference, would you mind? *(He takes Eric's seat at the piano)*

ERIC   Don't forget, for another £4 we could have had Ted Heath.

André plays the Grieg Piano Concerto perfectly. Eric looks askance at André, puts his hands in his pockets, and turns aside.

ERIC   Rubbish.

Eric and Ern leave the stage. André plays the same vamp as Eric had, they rush back on and dance as André vamps.

ERIC   That's it!

A LETTER FROM
André Preview

My relationship with Eric and Ernie is not the usual conductor-to-soloist relationship. While it is true that Eric did play the Grieg Piano Concerto for me, and while it is true that, during a return engagement, both the gentlemen sang while I conducted, it must be said that our pattern of work habits differs from the norm.

When we have the ordinary, run-of-the-mill soloist with the London Symphony Orchestra, we waste a lot of time at rehearsals talking about mundane, boring things such as the varying interpretive fine points of the repertoire, the musicological background of the work involved, opinions on phrasing and tempos, all that kind of unnecessary nonsense. On the other hand, I remember distinctly that during my first rehearsal with Eric and Ernie I spent quite a lot of the time defending myself, because I would not start the orchestra by going 'a-one, a-two'!! The rest of the rehearsal time was taken up by a discussion on the varying fine points of several ventriloquists we had all seen recently.

The boys have always been extremely kind and courteous to me. I want to give you an example of that: Eric never fails to apologise both before *and* after he hits me. I have been given to understand that they will ask me to work with them again, as soon as they can think of further humiliations to put me through. What's more, I look forward to it a great deal.

André Previn

Eric's DOG

Eric comes through the curtains and joins Ernie. Eric is holding a dog's lead that goes behind the curtains to a great height.

ERIC   (*Looking up*) Sit! Sit! Flamin' sit!!

ERNIE   He's a big dog.

ERIC   Enormous.

ERNIE   What breed is he?

ERIC   He's a guard dog.

ERNIE   What does he guard?

ERIC   High rise flats. Sit! Sit!!

ERNIE   What do you call him?

ERIC   Sir.

ERIC'S DOG.

118

ERN IN FRONT OF TABS.

ERN. Tonight we think that we've got a really specially guest for you on the show. This man is without doubt ...

ERIC THROUGH THE TABS WEARING OUTDOOR CLOTHING AND HOLDING A DOG LEASH WHICH TRAILS BACK THROUGH THE TABS.

ERIC. Just taking the dog for a walk.

ERN. I didn't know you had a dog.

ERIC. Only got him this afternoon. I bought it for protection at home

ERN. You need it these days.

ERIC. Yes. With any luck he might keep the wife from getting in.

ERN. Just take the dog for it's walk while I introduce the guest.

ERIC. The thing about this dog is ...

THE LEASH BEGINS TO RISE. IT GOES UP TO A GREAT HEIGHT

ERN. A dog''

ERIC. (LOOKING UP) Sit'' Sit''

THE LEASH TIGHTENS AND IT STARTS TO PULL ERIC ABOUT.

ERIC. (TO ERN) Don't just stand there8' Give me a hand''

ERN HOLDING THE LEASH AND BOTH BEING PULLED ABOUT.

ERN. What kind of a dog is it''

ERIC. Guard dog''

ERN. What does it guard?

ERIC. High rise flats'' Sit'' Sit''

BOTH BEING JERKED ABOUT.

ERN. It's enormous'

ERIC. Sit''Sit''

ERN. What do you call it?

ERIC. 'Sir' Keep hold of him' If he slips the lead he could demolish this place''

ERN. He seems a bit vicious'

ERIC. He'll like you once he gets used to your smell ... we all will. Sit'' Sit''

ERN. He must take a bit of feeding'

ERIC. I'll say he does'' Sit'' Sit''

ERN. How much meat does he eat in a day?

ERIC. What weight are you?

ERN. Ten and a half stone'

ERIC. That's about right'' Sit'' Sit''

LEASH LOWERS. STILL THE LEASH IS VERY TAUGHT AND BOTH HANGING ON

ERIC. S^ay'' Stay'' Watch out'' He's away''

BOTH ON THE FLOOR BY NOW AND BOTH ARE DRAGGED OFF UNDER THE TABS.

BOTH IN A Reflective MOOD

Do you remember our FIRST MEETING?

I DO. WE DECIDED TO TEAM UP AND HAVE A GO AT **COMEDY**

We should have **DONE**

Battle of the Poets

Eric: Dance to me my gypsy maid
       Dance as the firelight flickers
       Don't dance too close to the flames my dear
       You might set fire to your ...

Ernie: Don't! Don't you dare say it.

Eric: Cardigan! What's wrong with saying cardigan?

Ernie: You weren't going to say cardigan! You always say that
       you're going to say cardigan but you never do. You were
       going to say that word.

Eric: Which word?

Ernie: You're not going to fool me into saying it.

Eric: Cardigan! Nothing wrong saying cardigan.

Ernie: You never, ever say cardigan.

Eric: Only because you don't give me the chance, nothing
       untoward about saying cardigan.

Ernie: But you weren't going to say cardigan, you were
       going to say knickers.

Eric: Ha! Ha! You've said it. You dirty little
       devil.

Ernie: I hate you!

ERN AS Prime Minister Disraeli

ERIC AS Prince Albert

ERNIE I'm going to ratify my proposals.

ERIC I'll put the dog in the next room.

YOU AND LONG YOUR PAUSES

THAT WAS THE usual reaction from Eric and Ernie when the 'long pause' broke up the dialogue. They weren't keen at first on long pauses, but sometimes they do give greater impact to a comedy line – as I finally proved in a sketch that took place in the garden on a very hot summer's afternoon.

ERIC How many today?

ERNIE How many what today?

ERIC How may epic plays have you written today?

Pause while Ernie ponders.

ERNIE Twenty-seven epic plays.

ERIC And still only a quarter past ten.

Pause.

ERIC YOU COULD BE ANOTHER BRONTË SISTER YOU'VE GOT THE LEGS FOR IT

Another longer pause.

ERIC Ern.

ERNIE Yes?

ERIC Good.

Pause.

ERIC	The Bard.
ERNIE	Who?
ERIC	William Shakespeare.
ERNIE	Oh, The Bard.
ERIC	Barred from every pub in Stratford Uneven.

The sketch not only had the pauses but also the music of Delius. 'On Hearing the First Cuckoo in Spring' has long been one of my favourite pieces of music and it really works well, adding to the atmosphere of that beautiful afternoon, as did the pauses. Ernie is relaxing in a garden chair and listening to the music, which is coming from a portable radio on a wicker table. Eric enters wearing his famous shorts. He pauses for a moment taking in the atmosphere, the ambience of that memorable afternoon. I know that it all took place in a television studio and was only make-believe, but I'll never forget it. During the final dress rehearsal, quite extraordinarily, the studio seats were almost full of BBC staff, and it really was the norm when we got to a final dress rehearsal that all the seats were taken by staff sneaking off to watch the show. On this particular rehearsal word must have spread about the garden sketch because that was when almost every seat was taken. You can place your own pauses in this sketch.

Eric pauses again.

ERIC	Nice music.
ERNIE	Delius.
ERIC	Who's it by?
ERNIE	Delius. That's the composer's name.
ERIC	Was he British?
ERNIE	Who?

ERIC   Devious.

ERNIE   Delius.

ERIC   Was he British?

ERNIE   Bradford.

ERIC   Could have sworn he was British. Nice flowers.

ERNIE   Yes.

ERIC   The red ones, they geronimoes?

ERNIE   Geraniums.

That sketch ran for about seven or eight minutes. If they'd let me I could have got thirty minutes out of it, a situation comedy, although it was something I've never wanted to get involved in. A laugh every five minutes? I haven't got the patience. Which is why Eric and Ernie were so right for me, they worked at a hell of a lick.

ERNIE'S AWARD

The opening of a show. Ernie comes out front first and begins an introduction, Eric follows him on and interrupts. He calls for the curtains to be closed and pulls a chair from behind them. He seats Ernie, reaches behind the curtain again and brings out a large silver trophy. Ernie looks surprised and expectant.

ERNIE   This is a complete surprise to me, I don't know what to say.

ERIC   Ernest Oliver Toby Wise …

ERNIE   Is it *This Is Your Life*?

ERIC   No, it's better than *This Is Your Life*. Over the years … incidentally, anything is better than *This Is Your Life*. Over the years Ern, you have given a lot of pleasure to a lot of people. But the least said about that the better. I have been asked by the Guild of Television Producers, founded in 1546, if I'll come along here tonight and make this presentation to you for your outstanding contribution to the world of entertainment.

Ernie rises and begins a tap dance.

ERIC   Not for that rubbish. You were born, Ern … you were born, weren't you?

ERNIE   Yes.

ERIC   You were born with a gift that is given to very few men. Very few men, ladies and gentlemen, can put their legs at the back of their neck and whistle a selection from Gilbert and Sullivan. I have seen this boy do it – haven't I?

ERNIE   You have.

ERIC   And when he's done it he's frightened the life out of the dog, haven't you?

ERNIE   Yes.

ERIC   However, that apart, it is as an entertainer that we all know, love and respect you.

ERNIE   I do my best.

ERIC   There's no need to apologise. Few people, ladies and gentlemen, apart from myself, know that Ern did not have to enter the world of showbusiness, because he came from a very – you don't mind me saying this, do you?

ERNIE   What are you going to tell them?

ERIC   That you come from a very wealthy family. You see, it broke his father's heart when Ernie told him he was going to go on the stage and wouldn't be able to take over from him the general managership of the multi-storey knackers yard. That's true, isn't it?

ERNIE   Oh yes, yes. We have branches all over the continent.

ERIC   It's well known. Inter-knacker, isn't it?

ERNIE   Yes. But what about the award?

ERIC   I'm coming to that. It's beautiful, isn't it?

ERNIE   It's the finest I've ever seen.

ERIC   Over the years, Ern, your work has been of the very highest order. You have set a standard few men can compete with.

ERNIE   Well, one has a job to do.

ERIC   'One has a job to do!' Typical of the man. And you have done your job despite setbacks that would have lesser men crying 'Enough!' I'm talking about your accident.

ERNIE   It was nothing.

ERIC   'It was nothing!' he says. It could have proved fatal. That magic roundabout was going full pelt when you fell off. Why are you so modest?

ERNIE   You didn't have to bring that up. What about the award?

ERIC   I'm coming to that. Nobody knows, Ern, your worth, better than me. Many times we have been working together and something has gone wrong, but you saved the day. Quick as a flash, without thinking, you collapsed.

ERNIE   I'd rather not talk about that.

ERIC   I don't blame you.

ERNIE   What about the award?

ERIC   I'm coming to it, son. At the age of eighteen you proved yourself in the field, but she promised never to tell her mother. And that is what you get the award for. The moment we've all been waiting for ... I feel a lump in my throat right now.

ERNIE   Gosh!

ERIC   Ernest Burkinshaw Paddy Wise, on behalf of just about every television viewer in the country it gives me the very greatest personal pleasure to be able to present you with this luncheon voucher.

        Eric takes a piece of paper out of the trophy.

ERIC   Now whatever you do, don't eat that all now, save it till you get home. And save a piece for me.

ERNIE   But ... luncheon voucher? What about the cup?

ERIC   I won that.

ERNIE   You won it? What for?

ERIC   Telling lies.

ERIC THE PROTECTOR

THERE WERE TIMES in the relationship when I liked to show that Eric was not always having a go at Ernie. A good example came in the dialogue between them after Cliff Richard had made an impressive guest appearance.

ERNIE   Cliff surprised me in that play.

ERIC   I told him to be careful with that umbrella.

ERNIE   I meant he could really act. Just a little more style, a little more sophistication. And he could well be another me.

ERIC   Never!

ERNIE   No. I suppose you're right.

Sometimes when Ern was trying to convince a very unconvinced guest that the play what he wrote was a classic and every bit as good as 'Henry the Ninth,' the guest might use a word that Ern didn't understand and he would look to Eric for help, as he was his friend. Ern would look perplexed when asked by a guest, who needed convincing, 'Do you have a rough synopsis?' This would be followed by an embarrassed pause before Eric stepped in on the defensive and said, 'Not since he's been using the pink ointment.'

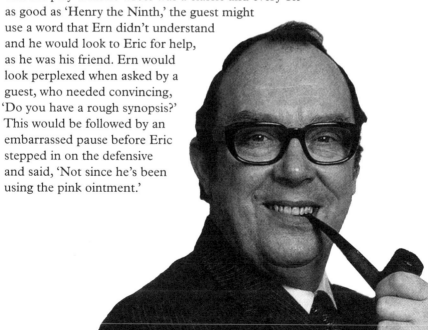

Ern would be very relieved at this timely intervention and would smilingly agree, 'That's perfectly true'.

As a matter of interest, when talking about ointment in British comedy, it always has to be pink – any other colour and the gag won't work, neither will the ointment. Take my experienced word for it, British audiences like their ointment pink.

Eric was always the protective shield against all those who dared to doubt Ern's work. As far as Eric was concerned, little Ern could do no wrong and he would stand by him at all times.

This was the case when Arthur Lowe had misgivings about 'Mutiny on the Bounty', Ern looking very uncomfortable at a guest finding a mistake in his work, so Eric stepped in.

ARTHUR   I think there's a typing error in the title.

ERIC   Typing error? That's 'Mutiny on the Bounty'.

ARTHUR   But he's put 'Monty on the Bonty'.

ERIC   That's not Ern's fault. No, no. That's a typing error due to the fact that his typewriter is made out of his old bike.

ARTHUR   Made a typewriter out of his bike?

ERIC   That's true. Now every time he cocks his leg over the ribbon he knocks the keys with his saddlebag.

Not really a lot you can say after that explanation.

How fortuitous that mistake turned out to be. It really was a typing error on my part. As I was typing out the 'Mutiny on the Bounty' dialogue I quite accidentally did hit the wrong key and printed out 'Monty' instead of 'Mutiny'.

How I wish I could have made a few more mistakes like that.

GOING FOR A QUICK ONE

ONCE AGAIN A prop featured strongly in this opening, which was an affectionate send-up of a very popular antiques programme of the day called *Des O'Connor*. No, that's not true. The programme was called *Going for a Song*. It was hosted by a very genial expert with a name I was more than grateful for: Arthur Negus, a very kind man who answered all the questions Eric and I put to him about clocks. We were both collectors. Eric was very enthusiastic when he told me about a clock he'd found half hidden away at the back of one of his favourite antique shops in Harpenden. The owner of the shop told Eric that the clock was over a hundred years old, but that it was also broken, black and rusty and he could have it for a fiver.

Eric bought it and told me with considerable pride that he had been working on the clock for a couple of hours a day for the past three weeks. 'You should see it now.' I was impressed and a touch jealous. When I asked 'What's it like?' he replied, 'Broken, black and rusty'. Incidentally, I put that line in about Des because I was astonished that we had done a routine about antiques without mentioning him. The Des O'Connor insult gags all came about because in the early days I was looking for the right personality for Eric to joke about, and it had to be someone who was very, very popular. I chose Des because at that time nobody was doing gags against him, he was one of the most popular entertainers in the business, my wife Dee adored him, and he sang! The very first in a catalogue of Des insult gags was, I think, this one.

ERIC: I'VE JUST BOUGHT DES O'CONNOR'S NEW ALBUM

ERNIE: WHERE FROM?

ERIC: BOOTS THE CHEMIST

ERNIE: DID YOU NEED A PRESCRIPTION?

ERIC: I HAD TO GO TO THE POISON COUNTER

That may or may not have been the first Des O'Connor insult gag. It certainly wasn't the last. When I eventually met Des he shook me warmly by the hand, not the throat, as I thought he might. He was very sincere when he thanked me, saying that it was publicity he could never have bought. Also that his family watched the shows and were very disappointed if Eric and Ernie didn't insult him. I don't think that they were ever disappointed. I'm quite sure that they weren't disappointed when all three finally came face to face.

ERIC   He's arrived.

ERNIE   Who?

ERIC   Do you scare easily?

ERNIE   I watch *Crossroads*.

ERIC   Then I can tell you that he's arrived.

ERNIE   Who?

ERIC   I'll give you just a little clue … Des O'Connor.

ERNIE   He's in the building?

ERIC   Yes.

ERNIE   Are you sure?

ERIC   When the guard dog tries to throw itself off the roof, Des O'Connor must be in the building.

ERNIE   He'll want to sing one of his songs.

ERIC   I want to marry Raquel Welch but some things just aren't possible.

ERNIE   God! He's coming!

ERNIE   Oh. Ladies and gentlemen, a great personal friend of ours, Des O'Connor.

ERNIE   Des, it's a joy to see you.

ERIC   Good old Des. Lovely to meet you at long last.

DES   Thank you, boys. I take it then that I am going to sing?

ERNIE   Sing?

DES   Yes. I'm going to sing.

FOR THE 1967 SUMMER SEASON

Leslie Grade in Association with ABC presents

ERIC MORECAMBE & ERNIE WISE

in

THE MORECAMBE & WISE SHOW

WITH **IVOR EMMANUEL**

DAVID & MARIANNE
DALMOUR

SAVEEN
ASSISTED BY DAISY MAY

ERIC DELANEY
AND HIS BAND

ANNA-LOU & MARIA

THE PAMELA
DEVIS DANCERS

JIMMY LEE
AVA KAY
MARGARET REDMOND

Devised and produced by ALBERT J. KNIGHT Choreography by Pamela Devis

ERIC   Well, with practise I'm sure one day you will.

Des, after some rather devious manoeuvres, did sing. It was a song from his one-man show, and it isn't easy singing a song with only one man in the audience. Time we joined Eric and Ernie's antique antics with Arthur Negus.

Eric is carrying a box made of antique-looking wood.

ERNIE   Good evening, ladies and gentlemen, and welcome to the show. What's in that box?

ERIC   He just gave it to me now.

ERNIE   Who?

ERIC   The antique expert in the next studio. Arthur Negligee.

ERNIE   You mean Arthur Negus.

ERIC   Yes, I was in the studio next door watching him doing his antique programme. Thought I might pick up a few jokes.

ERNIE   You're not short of antique jokes.

ERIC   Is that it?

ERNIE   So you met Arthur Negus.

ERIC   Yes, I always get confused between him and the one who married Herbert Wilcox.

ERNIE   Anna Neagle.

ERIC   I am glad ... Herbert Wilcox's wife Arthur Negus was in the studio next door, recording the antique programme *Going for a Quick One*.

ERNIE   *Going for a Song*.

ERIC   He sings as well? I didn't know that.

ERNIE   You're interested in antiques?

ERIC   You've seen the wife.

ERNIE   Arthur Negus was on the panel.

ERIC   Yes, but his doctor said he could work. Arthur looked at the first object and he said without a moment's hesitation, 'That statue is at least five hundred and sixty-seven years old.'

ERNIE   And was it?

ERIC   No. It was Max Robertson fast asleep in the chair.

ERNIE   Who was the guest celebrity?

ERIC   I'd rather not say because he did make a fool of himself and I don't wish to embarrass the man because I've nothing against Des O'Connor.

ERNIE   Was he any good?

ERIC   No idea about antiques. He looked at the object, smiled that smile of his, did forty-five songs and half a joke then said, 'I would say that this object is a pair of Stone Age jockey shorts.'

ERNIE   He guessed wrong?

ERIC   A mile out.

ERNIE   But the expert told him what it was.

ERIC   Yes, the expert – Arthur Nuisance.

ERNIE   Negus.

ERIC   He picked the object up and he said, almost with contempt, that expression on his face.

ERNIE   Wrinkles his nose up when he's looking at it.

ERIC   So do I.

ERNIE   What did he say it was?

ERIC   You'll be amazed when I tell you. It's in this box.

ERNIE   What is it?

ERIC   Only one of its kind left in the world.

ERNIE   What is it?

ERIC   You won't believe me when I tell you what this is.

ERNIE   What is it?

ERIC   Only one of its kind left.

ERNIE   You've said that. What is it?

ERIC   Would you like to know what it is? This, believe it or not, was made in the late seventeenth century. It is a genuine Jacobean TV set.

ERNIE   A Jacobean television set!

ERIC   Given to me by Arthur Nugget.

ERNIE   Anna Neagle … Can't you get anyone's name right?

ERIC   I'm sorry, Herbert.

ERNIE   That's a Jacobean television set?

ERIC   Yes.

ERNIE   I suppose you're going to tell me it's in working order?

ERIC   Do you know what I'm going to tell you?

ERNIE   No.

ERIC   It's in full working order. I'll show you. Switch on first. *(Presses button on front of set and raises aerial. Opens the little doors of the set: inside we see a picture of Eric and Ern.)* It's them again!

ERNIE   They're never off.

ERIC   I like the one with the glasses. I can't stand the other fellow.

ERNIE   They're good though, aren't they?

ERIC   One of them is.

        Exits with set.

Eric: Rubbish.

Ernie: What is?

Eric: Your poetry.

Ernie: You can do better?

Eric: I think so.

Ernie: Let's hear one of your poems.

Eric: Very well. I wrote this one for a get-well-soon card.

Ernie: Let's hear it.

Eric: I'm sorry to hear that you're not well,
        Soon you'll be full of life,
        Just take it easy and stay in bed,
        Like I am with your wife.

Ernie: That wasn't half bad.

Eric: Thank you.

Ernie: It was all bad.

Eric: Then how about …
        There was a young lady from Preston,
        Who ran down the M6 with no vest on,
        She was just outside Crewe when
        A sailor named Lou,
        Grabbed her ...

Ernie: I think we've all had enough of your mucky poems.

THIS IS YOUR LIFE

ERNIE

THAMES TELEVISION PLC
Broom Road, Teddington Lock,
Teddington, Middlesex.
Tel: 081-977-3252

C A M E R A   S C R I P T
****

R/T: 38'25"

WEDNESDAY 31 OCTOBER, 1990.

VTR/THS/52535

PN: L.5097

'JOIN'

THIS IS YOUR LIFE

'JOIN'

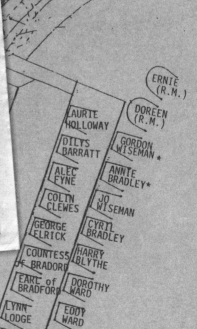

ERNIE
(R.M.)

DOREEN
(R.M.)

LAURIE
HOLLOWAY

GORDON
WISEMAN *

DILYS
BARRATT

ANNIE
BRADLEY*

ALEC
FYNE

JO
WISEMAN

COLIN
CLEWES

CYRIL
BRADLEY

GEORGE
ELRICK

HARRY
BLYTHE

COUNTESS
of BRADORD

DOROTHY
WARD

EARL of
BRADFORD

EDDY
WARD

LYNN
LODGE

MARTIN
CLARKSON

"THIS IS YOUR LIFE" 'JOIN'
WEDNESDAY 31 OCTOBER, 1990.

VTR/THS/ 52535
PN: L.5097

GUESTS IN ORDER OF APPEARANCE

LAURIE HOLLOWAY, DILYS BARRATT, ALEC FYNE,
COLIN CLEWES, GEORGE ELRICK, COUNTESS OF BRADFORD,
EARL OF BRADFORD, LYNN LODGE, MARTIN CLARKSON
JO WISEMAN, CYRIL BRADLEY, HARRY BLYTHE, DOREEN WISE.
MARTY CHRISTIAN, JILLY COOPER, DAVID LODGE, GEMMA CRAVEN,
GEORGE CHISHOLM, JUNE WHITEFIELD, LIONEL BLAIR, MARION MONTGOMERY,
MICHAEL BARRATT, SID GREEN, DICK HILLS, STEVEN HOCKRIDGE,
MURRAY HOCKRIDGE, JACKIE HOCKRIDGE, TED HOCKRIDGE, PHILLIP JENKINSON,
JOHN AMMONDS, EDDIE BRABEN, DEIDREE BRABEN, CLARE BRABEN, PHILIP JONES,
FLORENCE JONES, RICHARD WHITMORE, RICHARD BAKER, PETER WOODS.

Page No

ALREADY SEATED

GLENDA JACKSON	
DOROTHY & EDDY WARD	4
JACK BENTLEY	7
ANNIE BRADLEY & GORDON WISEMAN	11
CONSTANCE DAWSON _/VTR ONLY/_	12
JOAN MORECAMBE	14
ANGELA RIPPON	18
TEDDY JOHNSON & PEARL CARR _/VTR ONLY/_	20
SIR ROBIN DAY	22
SHIRLEY BASSEY _/VTR ONLY/_	24
PETER CUSHING	27
	31

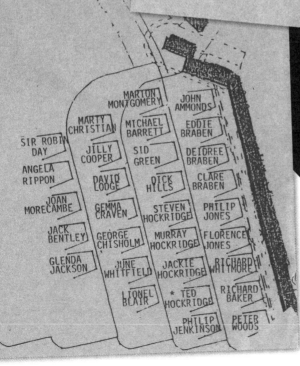

SE...
SE...

SIR ROBIN DAY — ANGELA RIPPON — JOAN MORECAMBE — JACK BENTLEY — GLENDA JACKSON

MARTY CHRISTIAN — JILLY COOPER — DAVID LODGE — GEMMA CRAVEN — GEORGE CHISHOLM — JUNE WHITFIELD — LIONEL BLAIR

MARION MONTGOMERY — MICHAEL BARRATT — SID GREEN — DICK HILLS — STEVEN HOCKRIDGE — MURRAY HOCKRIDGE — JACKIE HOCKRIDGE — * TED HOCKRIDGE — PHILIP JENKINSON

JOHN AMMONDS — EDDIE BRABEN — DEIDREE BRABEN — CLARE BRABEN — PHILIP JONES — FLORENCE JONES — RICHARD WHITMORE — RICHARD BAKER — PETER WOODS

ERNIE WAS THE SUBJECT OF THIS IS YOUR LIFE IN 1990. THE SEATING PLAN WAS ALMOST LIKE A WHO'S WHO OF MORECAMBE & WISE

ANTONY & CLEOPATRA

BY ERNEST WiSE

QUEEN CLEOPATRA: Glenda Jackson
MARK ANTONY: Ernie Wise
DESDEMONA: Ann Hamilton
OCTAVIAN CAESAR: Eric Morecambe

*Scene: A richly furnished apartment in Cleopatra's palace.
Main item of furniture is a divan piled high with cushions.
Across centre background are richly coloured curtains which,
when drawn back, would show a view of the desert Sphinx.
The curtains are closed at the back of the set.*

ANN   My Queen Cleopatra will be receiving Mark Antony soon.
(Begins to tidy cushions on divan) My queen is beautiful
but ruthless. Mark Antony loves her most dearly, like
all men he just melts before the fire of her beauty!
(Listens) My queen is here now!

*Glenda enters as Cleopatra and we hear signature music of
Dr Finlay's Casebook.*

Glenda looks puzzled. She raises her hand.

GLENDA   There you are, Desdemona.

ANN   My queen.

GLENDA   Has my lover arrived yet?

ANN   Which one?

GLENDA   What day is it?

ANN   Friday.

GLENDA   *(Looks at diary)* Mark Antony. Two 'til ten.

ANN   He loves you terribly.

GLENDA   I keep telling him that. All men are fools, Desdemona. They place themselves at my feet and I use them as stepping stones.

Trumpet – Roman fanfare.

ANN   It's Mark Antony, my queen.

GLENDA   Another stepping stone arriving. Go and help him up the steps, he's only got little legs.

ANN   He is here now. Mark Antony!

Ernie enters to signature tune of Z Cars, *looking puzzled. When he raises his hand the music stops. He crosses to Glenda on knees.*

ERNIE   My queen. *(Kisses Glenda's hand)* I search in vain for words adequate enough to describe your beauty.

GLENDA   Try.

ERNIE   How's this for starters? I have only loved like this once before. When I die you will find engraved upon my heart the words 'Cleopatra' and 'Barclays bank'.

GLENDA   I can honestly say that I've never heard such flattering words. Would you leave us, Desdemona?

ANN   My queen. *(Bows and exits)*

ERNIE	Alone at last! Get the grapes out and let's get at it!

He jumps at Glenda but she moves. Ernie lands on divan.

GLENDA	Are you quite sure that we are alone?
ERNIE	Of course we're alone.
GLENDA	I think not. For some time now I have had the feeling that we are being watched.
ERNIE	Impossible!
GLENDA	You think so?

Crosses to curtains centre background and pulls them back. We see Eric looking through the hole in the Sphinx where the face of the Sphinx should be.

ERNIE	Oh he's so far away. He can't see us from there.

Eric picks up a telescope. Glenda closes the curtains.

ERNIE	Who was that?
GLENDA	I believe him to be a Roman guard, a soldier sent to my palace by Julius Caesar with strict orders to watch me and the company I keep.
ERNIE	If Julius Caesar gets to know that you and I have been …
GLENDA	It would mean death for us both.
ERNIE	And that's not nice, is it?
GLENDA	Don't worry. I can deal with him.

Ann enters.

ANN	My queen! The Roman guard is here!

Eric enters to signature music of Match of the Day. *He is dressed as a gladiator and wearing Wellington boots and a busby. Fade music. Ann exits.*

ERIC   Evenin' all! Sorry I'm late only I've been irrigating the desert – takes a bit of doing on your own.

GLENDA   Is Caesar with you?

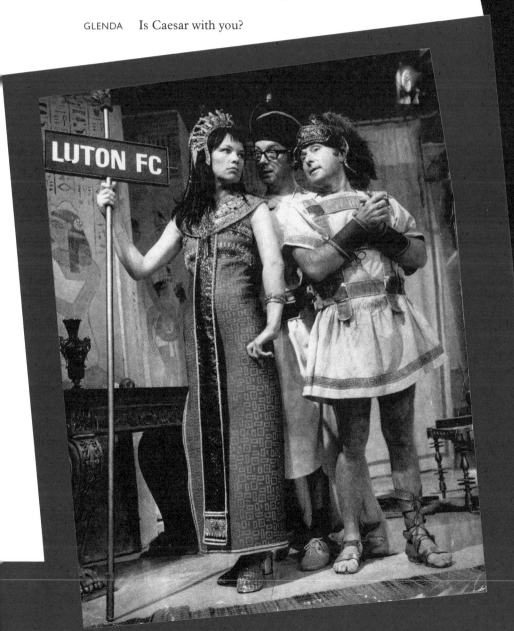

ERIC   No he couldn't come. He's got the hieroglyphics.

GLENDA   You must be hungry after such a long journey – can I get you some food?

ERIC   Thank you all the same but I've just had a couple of sheep's eyes – they'll see me through the day.

GLENDA   *(Seductively)* But you must be hungry for something.

ERIC   That's true.

ERNIE   And what is your business here?

ERIC   I have been sent from Julius and Caesar.

GLENDA   Julius and Caesar?

ERIC   I'm afraid so – a slight accident whilst polishing his sword.

GLENDA   Am I right in assuming that you have been sent here with the sole object of spying on me?

ERIC   Is there anything to spy on?

GLENDA   Meaning?

ERIC   You and the little chap here, have you been … touch of the hello folks.

ERNIE   Good heavens no, sir! How could you think such a thing! Nothing of that nature going on here I do assure you most sincerely.

GLENDA   All men are fools, and what makes them so is having beauty like what I have got.

ERNIE   You have a plan?

GLENDA   Let me have five minutes alone with him. If I can incriminate him we need have no fear of what he can do.

ERNIE He is a dedicated Roman soldier and you will never implicate him.

GLENDA Leave me alone with him.

ERNIE *(To Eric)* Would you like me to attend to your camel?

ERIC It's outside – can't miss it – looks like a horse with an airlock. *(Gives Ernie the hat)* Put this on his hump in case it freezes during the night.

ERNIE Right away! *(Exits)*

ERIC A remarkable beast.

GLENDA The camel?

ERIC No, Ern.

Oboe plays oriental music as Glenda moves seductively to the bed.

ERIC Is your back still bad?

GLENDA I like you.

ERIC Hello.

GLENDA You're a warm-blooded type and you're driving me mad with desire. I am aflame with passion and I can feel myself getting hotter every second.

ERIC Leave everything to me, cheeky.

He takes a frond to use as a fan. All leaves drop off as he shakes it.

GLENDA Is this your first visit to Egypt?

ERIC Never been here before in my life.

GLENDA When was that?

ERIC   I think we've turned over two pages. About two years ago.

Both look puzzled.

GLENDA   What do you think of the pyramids?

ERIC   Excellent – their last record was a belter.

GLENDA   *(Sits)* I'm sure that you'll find it more comfortable on these cushions next to me.

ERIC   *(Reads from scroll)* Lady, I must warn you that I am a soldier of Rome and that I have sworn a vow to my Emperor. If you are toying with the idea of trying to seduce me, I must tell you that I will have no alternative other than to leave this room first thing tomorrow morning – move up.

He sits next to Glenda. Glenda reaches for the grapes. Eric gets up with grapes and goes behind the bed. Puts grapes on the floor. Treads them quickly. Bends down and picks up a glass of wine.

ERIC   *(Gives Glenda the glass)* There you are.

GLENDA   Sit down.

ERIC   I am sat down.

GLENDA   Would you like to rest your head on my lap?

ERIC   If you can get it off, of course. *(Rests head on Glenda's lap)*

GLENDA   Don't you find the desert romantic?

ERIC   It's all right now but what's it like when the tide comes in?

GLENDA   I like you. Kiss me.

ERIC   Well all right then.

GLENDA   Comfortable?

ERIC   Just a minute. *(Reaches under cushions and brings out Glenda's Oscar)* Yours I believe?

Ernie enters with a pedestal. He kneels behind divan and rests his head on pedestal.

GLENDA   Sorry. *(Takes Oscar and places it to one side)* Now then … *(Begins to stroke Eric's hair. Ernie is watching, between them)* Do you like me stroking your hair?

ERIC   Don't stroke it too hard – I've only got four left and three of them are Ernie's.

ERNIE   *(To Glenda, through the side of his mouth)* Put the sleeping powder in his goblet.

GLENDA   *(Side of mouth)* I beg your pardon?

ERNIE   The sleeping powder in his goblet – then we can sling him in the Nile.

GLENDA   *(To Eric)* Oh, another drink?

She takes goblet from table and empties powder from ring. Eric listens. Glenda turns and gives the goblet to Eric. She turns back to the table to get her own drink. Eric throws contents over his shoulder into Ernie's face. Ernie does business of going to sleep.

GLENDA   How long is it since you last saw a woman?

ERIC   I've forgotten, sir! *(He tries to free himself from Glenda)*

GLENDA   *(Holding Eric down)* It's no use trying to fight me. I can feel your heart pounding like a whippet inside a bowler hat.

ERIC   *(Rises quickly)* Oh, but you are having an affair with Mark Antony.

GLENDA   *(Rises in anger)* Me and Mark Antony? Don't mention that man's name to me. I can't stand the sight of him!

ERNIE   *(Out from behind pedestal in anger)* I heard that! I heard what you said about me and I'm not having that! It's time for me to act.

GLENDA   That'll be the day.

ERIC   You loved this lady?

ERNIE   I loved her once.

ERIC   Once? I thought you were a centurion. You're all talk you are.

GLENDA   Mark Antony, you have been and always will be a fool!

ERNIE   You've been using me as a big prawn!

ERIC   You can't fight nature.

GLENDA   *(Arms around Eric's neck)* I love you and I want you to take me with you to Rome.

ERNIE   She lies! And what makes her so is having beauty like what she has got.

Ann rushes on.

ANN   My queen.

GLENDA   What is it Desdemona?

ERIC   Desdemona? She looks more like Des O'Connor.

ANN   My queen, terrible news from abroad.

ERIC   I knew it, they want the Oscar back.

GLENDA   Speak, Desdemona.

ANN   If you return to Rome with that man you will die.

GLENDA	Is this true?
ERIC	As surely as the desert sun rises above the Co-op in Cairo.
GLENDA	Who are you?
ERIC	I am Octavian Caesar. Nephew of Julius and Caesar. Ruler of all the world including parts of Birkenhead.
ERNIE	Julius Caesar's nephew? I can't believe it.
ANN	Now do you see why he wants to take you back to Rome?
GLENDA	As his prisoner – to face Julius and Caesar and certain death.
ERIC	*(To Ernie)* You have been having an affair with the queen!
GLENDA	It was nothing!
ERIC	I can believe that!
GLENDA	Then you intend seeing this through to the bitter end?
ERIC	Might as well, we've learned all the words.
GLENDA	I have one final request.
ERIC	Well hurry up because we're running late.
ERNIE	A final request?
GLENDA	If I am to die I'd like to do it by my own hand.
ANN	*(Sobbing)* No!
ERIC	A fine actor, that boy. Another contract.
GLENDA	Fetch me the asp.

Ann gets a basket from the side. She puts it down and exits sobbing.

GLENDA   This is the end for me.

ERIC   She's got an asp in that basket.

GLENDA   Would you hold the basket while I remove the lid? This deadly serpent will put an end to my misery by biting me on the breast.

Eric takes the basket, and both he and Ernie react.

ERIC   Could I have a word with you please? *(They whisper)*

GLENDA   *(Parts her dress at the top and closes her eyes for the 'bite')* End it for me now! *(Eric's hand comes snake-like out of the top of the basket)*

ERNIE   What are you doing?

ERIC   Just warming the snake up.

ERNIE   You're disgusting you are!

ERIC   Of course I am!

GLENDA   *(Eyes still closed)* Put me out of my misery.

ERIC   Any second now. Ready?

WHAT iS iT DESDEMONA?

DESDEMONA? SHE LOOKS MORE LIKE DES O'CONNOR.

GLENDA   Ready!

Glenda starts to die.

ERIC   No, too early! Now!

Eric's snake-like hand bites Glenda and she dies a slow death on the cushions.

ERIC   Is she dead?

ERNIE   Yes.

ERIC   Good, now's me chance. *(Takes the Oscar from behind cushions)* I'm going to pinch her Oscar.

ERIC   Happy with that play, Ern?

ERNIE Perfectly. It was beautifully written.

ERIC And Glenda?

ERNIE Quite happy. She came up to my expectations.

ERIC You were standing on a box.

ERNIE What an actress.

ERIC Glenda has that … I'm not sure what you call it but it's caused through sleeping with a tight hairnet on.

ERNIE On an equally serious note I did change my style of writing for the next play.

ERIC If I remember rightly you didn't so much change your style of writing as your position because of the rash.

ERNIE That had nothing to do with it. I used a completely new technique in my play which took a look at what our future might be in a work of mine called *Ten Years Hence*.

ERIC I remember that play. You were nominated for that one. I would have done it myself if I could have found a chisel.

ERN'S BIRTHDAY

ERIC AND ERN ENTER THROUGH TABS.

ERN. Good evening, ladies and gentlemen, welcome to the show. Good audience tonight, Eric.

ERIC. Intelligent.

ERN. Intelligent?

ERIC. Half of them are leaving.

ERN. Ladies and gentlemen ..

ERIC. Novelty night tonight.

ERN. Novelty night?

ERIC. For the first time ever on British Television my associate here is going to play four trumpets at the same time - three of them with his mouth. Do they know that you're in The Guinness Book of Records?

ERN. It doesn't matter.

ERIC. He's a book mark.

ERN. Tonight ..

ERIC. Ern (OFFERS ERN A TELEGRAM) Many happy returns of the day. There's a telegram from the Queen

ERN. You've actually remembered my birthday?

ERIC. Am I a man to forget? Could I ever forget? (SINGING QUICKLY) Happy birthday to you, happy birthday to you, happy birthday dear ... dear (TRYING TO REMEMBER) Happy birthday dear ..

ERN. Ern.

ERIC. (SINGING) Dear Ern, happy birthday to you.

ERN. I'm more than a little touched.

ERIC. I've always thought that. From me to you (BIRTHDAY CARD)

ERN. A birthday card for me?

ERIC.   If I might read the verse? (READING FROM CARD) A happy birthday,
        dear Ern, your age I will not mention, at least you won't have to
        work so hard now that you can collect your Old Age Pension

ERN.   Did you buy me a present?

ERIC.   It's a surprise. The great man is another year older.

ERN.   But I've still got the same enthusiasm and the same talent.
        ERN SHORT DANCE AND SINGING. STOPS AND IS OUT OF BREATH.

ERIC.   Now that you've got the wrinkles out of your Long John's ...
        how old are you?

ERN.   Famous and popular stars don't go around letting the people know
        how old they are.

ERIC.   I'm not asking a famous and popular star. I'm asking you.

ERN.   My age is my business

ERIC.   Are you between 24 and 126?

ERN.   I'm not telling you how old I am

ERIC.   Is it true that during the war you were scarred on the left
        shoulder by the spear of a Fuzzy-Wuzzy? And while in the Field
        Hospital you complained about the big lump in the mattress.
        Florence Nightingale said "If that's the way you feel I'll go back
        to my own bed"

ERN.   Stop talking nonsense. How did you know it was my birthday anyway?

ERIC.   By chance I came across a photograph of you, cut with loving care
        from a copy of 'The Mousebreeders Weekly' by your mother. On the
        back was written 'Little Ern on his twelfth birthday making his
        first stage appearance'

ERN.   Me at the age of twelve? Gosh'
        ERIC GETS PICTURE OF SHIRLEY TEMPLE FROM BEHIND CURTAINS AND
        SHOWS IT TO THE AUDIENCE, ERN DOES NOT SEE IT, THEN PUTS IT BACK
        BEHIND THE CURTAINS.

ERN.   I didn't see anything. Why did they laugh? Was it the photo where
        I was wearing the sailor suit?

ERIC.   You were heading that way.

ERN.   I could move in those days.

ERIC.   You probably had to

ERN.   And I can still go a bit now
        ANOTHER SHORT DANCE AT SPEED. ERN EVEN MORE OUT OF BREATH.

ERIC.   Silly old fool! The glue will start running again.

ERN.   (GASPS) I've lost me puff.

ERIC.   That's a relief.

ERN.   You can make fun of me but I've worked with some of the all time
        greats.

ERIC.   Good Old Days?

ERN.   I'll say.

ERIC.   Are you still seeing her? You have worked with some very famous
        people, I know that. Diana Dors, Vera Lynn, Petula Clark.

ERN.   Big draws.

ERIC.   You probably knew them better than I did.

ERN.   What about my present?

ERIC.   It's a surprise. I envy you, because behind every successful man
        there's a woman.

ERN.   My wife.
        ERIC GETS PICTURE FROM BEHIND CURTAINS OF "GIANT HAYSTACKS"

ERN.   My wife is a woman and a half.

ERIC.   At least. You come from a very talented family.

ERN.   I'll say. I take after my father, it's in the blood.
        ERIC GETS PICTURE OF "COUNT DRACULA"

ERIC.   You've been honoured by Her Majesty for your services.

ERNIE

I'M MORE THAN A LITTLE TOUCHED

ERIC

I'VE ALWAYS THOUGHT THAT

ERN. Proudest moment of my life that was. I'll never forget standing outside Buckingham Palace all dressed up for that great occasion. ERIC GETS PICTURE OF "WORZLE GUMMIDGE" (3)

ERIC. You were very lucky because you had a very good agent.

ERN. He was the best! He knew all the tricks my agent. They tried to con him and they finished up being conned. Dead cunning he was. ERIC GETS PICTURE OF HAROLD WILSON.

ERN. What about my present?

ERIC. It's a 'Surprise Party' being held at a big posh house.

ERN. Surprise party at a big posh house! Great! All laid on?

ERIC. It could turn out that way. All the food and drink you want - and it's free.

ERN. Where is this party?

ERIC. Here's the address (HANDS ERN PIECE OF PAPER)

ERN. This is my address!

ERIC. I told you it would be a surprise.

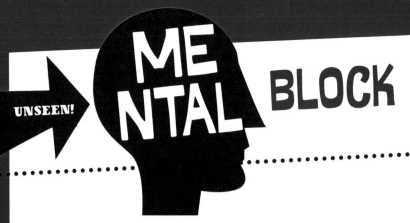

MENTAL BLOCK

Mental block, is that a condition or a residential home?

It happens frequently to me and I have to drill a way through to get at the words – as in this case.

Ernie: Eric.

Eric: Have been all day. I could change it.

Ernie: I'm being serious. I'm very worried.

Eric: I can see you're worried from the way you're walking. Do you need new batteries?

Ernie: Will you listen to me and stop doing jokes.

Eric: Of course. A couple of double 'A' batteries should do it because you've only got little legs. I'll put them in, not proud.

Ernie: Please listen.

Eric: After all, I did offer to shave your legs when you had that back problem and you couldn't reach.

Ernie: I'm worried and very upset and I think you know why.

Eric: Sorry about your goldfish. I honestly didn't know that the cat could swim.

YOU CAN'T GO wrong with a ventriloquist's doll. When the vent doll is ten feet tall it's got to be hilariously funny – and it was on this occasion when Eric came through those famous curtains carrying Oggy, a ten-foot vent doll. Ern looked on in total disbelief.

I've slightly rewritten this sketch, forgetting some of the original, in the hope that any new lines get laughs. Always hoping for laughs.

Ernie looks at Oggy in astonishment.

ERNIE   Good Lord!

ERIC   I couldn't get the big one.

ERNIE   The size of it.

ERIC   They all say that.

ERNIE   I've never seen anything like it.

ERIC   I'm very proud of Oggy.

ERNIE   Oggy?

ERIC   That's his name; I made him myself out of four sheds.

ERNIE   Can't be easy holding up four sheds.

ERIC   Four talking sheds.

ERNIE   Solid wood?

ERIC   His mother was a pole.

ERNIE   Make him talk.

ERIC   I can't.

ERNIE   Why not?

ERIC   His thing is too high up.

ERNIE   What thing?

ERIC   The thing you pull to make his mouth open.

ERNIE   Well, jump up and pull it.

ERIC   No. You'll have to wait until after the watershed.

ERNIE   Where did you get him from?

ERIC   Do you know that clearing in Epping Forest? That's him.

ERNIE   Has he got a good finish?

ERIC   He's French polished and you can't get them better than that.

ERNIE   Is he lacquered?

ERIC   He's bound to be! He's worked hard!

CAST

ERIC MORECAMBE
ERNIE WISE
GEMMA CRAVEN
HANNAH GORDON
DERYCK GUYLER (walk-on)
KAREN ALEXANDER (warm-up artist)
BILL MARTIN (warm-up artist)

...CREW

.........SUZANNE WESTON
.........TONY TYRER
.........BETTY CROWE
.........RUTH HALLIDAY
.........FRAN BOLWELL
.........CHRISTINE MORRELL
.........PETER LE PAGE
.........JEROME GASK
.........DEL RANDALL
.........JOHN DARNELL
.........MALCOLM HARRISON
.........DICK BRADFORD
.........PAUL GARTRELL
.........ALLAN JAMES
.........NICK BIGSBY

...L REQUIREMENTS

...MACHINE TO RECORD
...MACHINE TO SLAVE
...MACHINE TO PLAYBACK

...EDULE
...era Rehearsal..................1130 - 1330
...unch Break......................1330 - 1430
...amera Rehearsal.................1430 - 1600
...amera Break....................1600 - 1645
...Line Up/Make up.................1645 - 1815
...Dress Rehearsal................1815 - 2000
...Supper Break...................2000 - 2130
...Line up/Make up................2130 - 2145
...VTR...........................
...Tech. Clear...................

The tea trolley will be in
the Green Room at 1600.

MORECAMBE & WISE - Show 6   P/N: L 3406
RECORDING ORDER   VTR/22378

SKETCHES	CHARACTERS	CAMS	SHOTS	SOUND	PAGES
1. Opening titles on VTR		VTR			
2. OPENING DOUBLE	ERIC ERNIE KAREN ALEXANDER	1,2,3,4,	2-24	BOOM ¼" tape	1-10

T A P E   S T O P - Eric/Ern change for Foreign Legion

DURING TAPE STOP PLAY-IN AND RECORD VTR QUICKIES (from Show 5)

1) Insert 2 - The Window Cleaner
2) Insert 3 - The Milkman
3) Insert 4 - The Legionaires

| 3. THE FOREIGN LEGION | ERIC ERNIE | 2,3,4 | 25-46 | BOOM ¼" Tape | 11-16 |

T A P E   S T O P - Eric/Ern change for Flat Sketch

DURING TAPE STOP PLAY-IN AND RECORD VTR QUICKIES (from Show 5)

4) Insert 5 - Mastermind
5) Insert 6 - Pipe tobacco commercial
6) Insert 7 - Marlene Dietrich

| 4. FLAT SKETCH The Au Pair | ERIC ERNIE GEMMA CRAVEN | 1,2,3 | 47-96 | BOOM | 17-33 |

T A P E   S T O

| 5. CLOSING ROUTINE | ERIC ERNIE GEMMA | | | | |
| 6. VTR - Dance No. | | | | | |

T A P E   S T O P

RECORDING ORDER (con't)

SKETCH	CHARACTERS	CAMS	SOUND	SHOTS	PAGES
7. CLOSING ROUTINE Show 2	ERIC ERNIE DERYCK GUYLER	1,2,3,4	BOOM	99	35-36

T A P E   S T O P - Eric/Ern change for closing show 3
(Hannah Gordon)

| 8. CLOSING ROUTINE Show 3 | ERIC ERNIE HANNAH GORDON | 1,2,3,4, | BOOM ¼" Tape | 100 | 37-38 |

T A P E   S T O P

THE END!

Partytime!

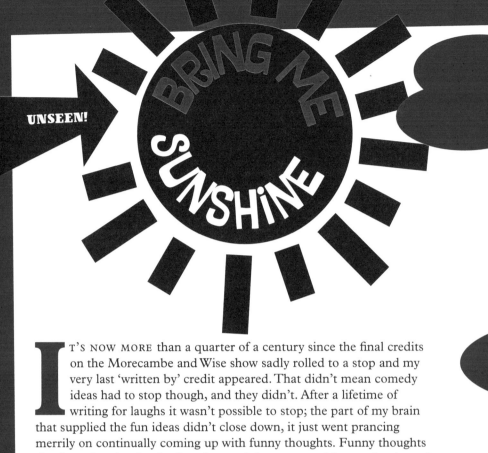

IT'S NOW MORE than a quarter of a century since the final credits
on the Morecambe and Wise show sadly rolled to a stop and my
very last 'written by' credit appeared. That didn't mean comedy
ideas had to stop though, and they didn't. After a lifetime of
writing for laughs it wasn't possible to stop; the part of my brain
that supplied the fun ideas didn't close down, it just went prancing
merrily on continually coming up with funny thoughts. Funny thoughts
that I was hearing for the first time and they were making me laugh, and
I freely and honestly admit that I always laughed at my own jokes, very
often the only one who did.

Unfortunately, despite all of these new ideas, this new comedy had
nowhere to go.

Hardly a day has passed since 1983 when I haven't had a head full of
jokes with no home to go to; they've just floated off unlaughed at. A joke
with no home to go to is a criminal waste in a world needing fun, and I

couldn't allow that to happen. I may well be a resident of Jurassic Park but I still need to make people laugh. I didn't want to waste my words so I started putting them down on paper. My hope was that when my canary stopped singing my family for generations to come would find them funny and remember how it used to be performed to perfection by two dear friends of mine called Eric and Ernie. When I did put all those words down it was sad because there wasn't anyone, so far as I knew, who could perform them. No matter how good they were, they would never be accepted with the same warmth and affection.

It was then that I realised why I was laughing at these new words. It was because I could see them – Eric and Ern – inside my head. In my imagination they were performing just as they always did, and it was beautiful. I hope you will enjoy the same experience as I did. Build your own scenery, choose the wallpaper in the flat and decide what colour pyjamas they'll be wearing in the bed sketch. If I'm living in the past then I'd very much like you to join me. It really is a fun place and the people are quite delightful. I just had to write the following pages. It's what I do.

One of the questions that I was most often asked when touring the country in my one-man show was: 'Where's the exit?'

Second most asked: 'Is it half price for OAPs?'

'Yes.'

'Good. I'll come back in forty years.'

Now that I've got those two lines out of my system, let me tell you the question I'm asked more than any other:

'Do you have a favourite sketch?'

Yes I do, and without hesitation it has to be the bed sketch. If I'd had my way every show would have been an hour-long bed or flat sketch. With those sketches we were doing a situation comedy within the framework of a light entertainment show; some of those bed and flat sketches lasted twenty minutes.

The reason why I was so fond of the bed sketch was that it brought the two of them as close together as it's possible to bring any two human beings. The bed was like a horse skin, no escape. They were closeted together and it was a joy for me to write, as it was truly undiluted Morecambe and Wise. It was also very difficult to get the idea of two men sharing a bed accepted in 1980. At one point, I was in danger of losing the idea completely. How could Eric and Ernie sharing a bed be looked on as anything other than Eric and Ern playing it for laughs? I couldn't understand why the men in grey suits had doubts.

I hope you like this one.

NOCTURNAL *Frolics*

UNSEEN!

H E WAS SITTING up in bed propped on pillows, with notepad and pen. He pondered then wrote, pondered then wrote. Those of you who are familiar with the words of this great author will not be surprised to learn that his brain was so sharp that he pondered little, but wrote furiously, and even at this late hour – it had just turned half past nine – he was completely and totally focused on his writing. Eric entered wearing a dressing gown over his pyjamas.

'Ern?'

'Yes?'

'I'm just checking. You never know these days. I could have found myself in bed with a Cyril.'

'Eric, please don't do the jokes. Just let me get on with my writing. This is a very important work.'

'All your works are important. I don't know how you do it,' said Eric as he climbed into bed. 'You just go on and on writing non-stop. You're like a human ballpoint pen. You'll never run out of words.'

'I was born to write.'

'I know that, Ern. I won't bother you. I respect what you do. Not another word.'

'Good,' Ern said and he pondered.

'Are you doing it now?'

'Doing what now?'

'Writing.'

'I'm trying to think. Fat chance of writing anything with you in this mood.'

'Sorry,' said Eric as he picked up a puzzle magazine from the bedside table. Obviously he didn't reckon much to the publication as he very quickly turned page after page making sure that each page made a noise. He was trying not to laugh, and Ern was getting slightly agitated.

'Must you make that noise?'

'It's not compulsory. I'm just looking for a page.'

'You're trying to annoy me.'

'That's true,' said Eric. 'I can do both.'

There was a slight lull which wasn't going to last because Eric was in one of his restless moods. He watched Ern as he wrote in his notepad and looked slightly puzzled at something that he had just written. 'What's that word?'

'It's a name.'

'A girl's name? There's no F in Phoebe. You've spelt Phoebe with an F. Seventy-eight awards, not to mention a shelf full of BAFTAs, and you can't spell Phoebe.'

'You mind your own business! Just shut up and give me a bit of peace.'

Which Eric did, for about ten seconds! 'The Salvation Army called this afternoon. They wanted to know if I could give them anything for the old folks' home.'

'I hope that you did give them something.'

'I couldn't.'

'Why not?'

'You were out.'

Ern was almost pleading. 'Eric will you please, please shut up and let me work. This work is very important to me. I'm acclaimed I am.'

'I don't know how you do all this writing. It's a gift not given to many, Ern.'

'How very true,' said Ern lowering his notepad. 'Yes. I must stop being so modest and admit that I am hugely gifted as an author. Not like me to boast.'

'You don't have to convince me, Ern. How many books have you written this week? Be honest, how many books have you written this week?'

Ern looked thoughtful before answering. 'Erm ... four. Four books this week.'

'Good Lord,' said Eric with some astonishment. 'Four books in a week and it's only Monday. How about the one that you wrote, the one that you wrote while you were waiting in the queue for the checkout at Tesco's?'

'That was only a short story,' said Ern, modestly. 'This will be my best work yet,' he said holding the notepad up, 'My autobiography. I'm writing it myself.'

'Not many celebrities write their own life stories,' said Eric.

Ern was surprised, 'Why not?'

'I'll tell you why not Ern. They haven't got your gift. They'd have to get a proper writer to do it for them. Some of your celebrities couldn't leave a note for the milkman. If they did they'd probably spell pint with a Y.'

'That's really surprised me,' said Ern. 'Spelling has always been one of my strong points. I always got ten out of ten for my spelling at school.'

'What are you going to call your autobiography?'

'I'm going to call it ...' he wrote on his notepad then read aloud ... 'Little Ern. The Story of a Legend.'

Eric took the notepad from Ern and looked at it admiringly. 'Very true, that title says it all about you, but there is just one thing and I hope you don't mind me saying this because I don't want to offend you.'

'You won't offend me, you have an opinion and I'd be happy to listen to it. What's wrong with the title?'

Eric looked at the notepad again. 'It's just that you've spelt Ern with a U.'

'I haven't spelt Ern with a U! I know how to spell my own name. It's just you, as usual, having a go at me because I'm writing the story of my life.'

'Ern, you did ask me.'

'And I'm only little. You're always picking on me.'

'Ern. I was joking.'

'You're always joking. Couldn't you just for once stop doing jokes?'

'That wouldn't be easy,' said Eric. 'I've always done jokes. It's the way I am, it's what I do. And look at me when I'm being serious. Could you stop writing?'

Ern thought about this and said, 'Could Mozart stop dancing?' Eric realised the stupidity of his question; had he been able to he would have taken a step back and kicked himself. It was time to try and make amends.

'You could never stop writing, not with your talent. I```n my opinion you could be another J.K. Rowlings.'

'I don't write gardening books.'

'It wouldn't surprise me,' said Eric, 'if the big studios wanted to make a film of your life.'

'I never thought of that!' Ern was excited at the thought. 'Yes why not? Be a great film. I wonder who they'd get to play me? Tom Cruise? He'd be great playing me. I'd let Tom be me.'

Eric looked surprised. 'Tom Cruise? I don't think so.'

'Why not? Tom Cruise, he's a fine actor, very good-looking, and perfect to play me.'

'No' said Eric. 'I don't think that Tom Cruise would do you justice. He hasn't got your charisma. Let's face it, you've got more than your share of charisma.'

Ern nodded in agreement. 'True. Who do you think would be good enough to play me?'

Eric looked thoughtful for a few seconds then said 'Bonnie Langford.'

'Bonnie Langford!?!' Ern couldn't believe what he'd just heard. 'Bonnie Langford! Bonnie Langford play the part of me!'

Eric's smile became a laugh when he said, 'She could play you to a T Ern – Tea urn! And she walks like you.'

Ern was furious. 'That's typical of you, that is! Typical! You haven't got any talent at all and you're jealous. You, you are a waste of time and space. You're hopeless!'

Eric: 'You may well be right, Ern, but I'll tell you something, I know how to spell Phoebe. Goodnight, Tom.'

FINAL
WORDS

ERIC   I ENJOYED **THAT.**

ERNIE   SO DID I.

ERIC   THAT'S ALL WE **EVER** WANTED.

ERNIE   IT'S BEEN FUN.

ERIC   JUST THE **TWO** OF **US.**

Pause.

ERNIE   ERIC, WHAT WOULD YOU DO WITHOUT ME?

Pause.

ERIC   BUY A **HAMSTER.**

PiCTURE CREDITS

The author and publishers have made every reasonable effort to contact all copyright holders. Any errors that may have occurred are inadvertent and anyone who for any reason has not been contacted is invited to write to the publishers so that a full acknowledgement may be made in subsequent editions of this work.

Images courtesy of: Page 7 Collection of Eddie Braben, 9 Collection of Eddie Braben, 10 Associated News, 12 BBC Publicity, 15 Collection of Eddie Braben, 18 Associated News, 20 Associated News, 26 Associated News, 34 Associated News, 42 Associated News, 47 Associated News, 54 Associated News, 57 Associated News, 62 Associated News, 67 BBC Publicity, 71 UCL Archive, 75 Associated News, 77 Associated News, 83 Collection of Eddie Braben, 90 UCL Archive, 98 Associated News, 102 Collection of Eddie Braben, 102 Collection of Eddie Braben, 107 Collection of Eddie Braben, 108 Associated News, 120 Associated News, 122 Associated News, 124 Associated News, 128 UCL Archive, 134 Collection of Eddie Braben, 136 Collection of Eddie Braben, 140-141 Collection of Eddie Braben, 145 Associated News, 151 Associated News, 154 Associated News, 156 Collection of Eddie Braben, 156 Collection of Eddie Braben, 157 Associated News, 163 Collection of Eddie Braben, 164 UCL Archive, 166 Collection of Eddie Braben, 170 Associated News, 174 Associated News, 176 Collection of Eddie Braben. Incidental images courtesy of Shutterstock.
All scripts courtesy of Eddie Braben.

ROLLER CAPTION.

CAPTAIN BASIL	......	TREVOR EVE.
BEAU GESTE	......	ERIC MORECAMBE.
BEAU LEGS	......	ERNIE WISE.
BEAU TIE	......	ROBIN DAY.
LOST PATROL LEADER	......	ROY JENKINS.
LEGIONNAIRE'S FRIEND	....	JOHN INMAN.
BELLY DANCER	......	CYRIL SMITH.
PARCHMENT SALESMEN	......	LITTLE & LARGE.
ROYAL ADVISOR	......	WILLIE HAMILTON.
HIRED ASSASSIN	......	EDWARD HEATH.
TEMPLE VIRGIN	......	ELIZABETH TAYLOR.
ARAB TRIBE	......	BARBARA CARTLAND.
ORIENTAL BEAUTY	......	HYLDA OGDEN.

A VIDEO CASSETTE OF THIS PLAY CAN NOW BE OBTAINED ON PRODUCTION OF A CERTIFICATE SIGNED BY TWO DOCTORS.